D1495442

37 YEARS OF
PUBLIC SERVICE

37 YEARS OF PUBLIC SERVICE

THE HONORABLE LYNDON B. JOHNSON

BY
JOE B. FRANTZ

SHOAL CREEK PUBLISHERS, INC.
P. O. BOX 968,   AUSTIN, TEXAS   78767

Library of Congress Catalog Card Number: 73-91025

Lithographed and Bound in the United States of America

"HONORABLE FAVORS . . ."

In the early 1930's, when the country was poor and night football was but a dream, Jesse Kellam was officiating a high school game in Corpus Christi, Texas. It was the afternoon before the big gas well blew in at Corpus and caught fire with a great rumble.

As a competent official, young Kellam ignored off-field sounds. But one insistent calling of his name caused him to turn around to find his former schoolmate, now a congressional secretary, a two-by-scantling stringbean named Lyndon Johnson. That night Kellam stayed in Corpus with Johnson, neither the first nor the last person to talk with the voluble young man until 3 o'clock in the morning. Some time during the long night, Johnson asked Kellam, "What do you want to do?" When Kellam told him, Johnson said, "What have you done about it?" And Kellam replied, "Not anything." Johnson said, "Well, let's get started tomorrow." Kellam then asked Johnson about his own future, to which Johnson answered promptly,

"I'm going to stay in public life."

"In politics?"

"Call it that if you want to," replied Johnson.

"What is your political philosophy?" asked Kellam.

The lad studied awhile and then replied carefully.

"Never pass up an opportunity to do an honorable favor for an honest friend."

For the next forty years Lyndon Baines Johnson followed this philosophy. Followed and honed and polished and deepened and broadened. Almost always in motion, he accomplished several lifetimes of work and service—looking after himself, his family, his district, his state, his nation, and the world.

To perpetuate the cliche', he hit the ground running, and he slowed only at the end. Few people had a greater time-and-work compulsion, and most of the time he had the physical resources to match his perpetual drive. During his public career he would never admit he was tired, no matter how long the day or how tense the situation, for he believed that once you admitted weariness to yourself or to others, you were finished. And so he pushed himself, pushed beyond other men's limits, and yet somehow always seemed to have more in reserve.

The result of these four decades of cascading energy, invariably with purpose, was a career that led from the dusty streets of Johnson City to the polished halls of history. Along the way Lyndon Johnson disturbed sleeping dogs, rattled old bones, changed people's rhythms, stretched others who wanted to remain rigid, and generally moved political and other mountains. Naturally he irritated people who wanted to leave well enough alone, who wanted to back up, or who wanted to pursue different trails. A man who never admits he's tired can be downright annoying, and Johnson undoubtedly annoyed many people as he worked at his myriad concerns.

But through all this purposeful push Johnson found highways that enabled him to reach out to friends and foes alike and do honorable favors for honest friends at levels from the precinct to the Presidency. He had more great moments than most men even aspire to, along with his quota of those that were tense or disappointing.

To tie down Johnson with one label is to misread his whole career. He was the bright and rising Congressman, the skillful Senate Majority Leader, the faithful Vice President, the Education President, the Civil Rights President, the Vietnam President, the Medicare President, and on and on. With his devout belief in results, he improvised, changed course, and generally disdained rigid doctrine. And so, all those persons of whatever political and/or philosophical persuasion who prefer stern doctrinal adherence, even if it means stalling in neutral, were often uneasy and incapable of grasping the essential quality of a man who believed that some progress was better than no progress; that there were no real enemies, but only people who hadn't yet been convinced; and that the nation and the world were large enough to accommodate men of all hues—physically, financially, politically, philosophically, and psychologically.

With such a near case of perpetual motion, to pinpoint how Lyndon Baines Johnson served in each year of his public life becomes a labor of deletion. Although the early years are naturally thinner than the later ones, even the yearling era adumbrates the powerful, all-encompassing future.

Therefore I have perforce proceeded arbitrarily, choosing here, ignoring or eliminating there. Anyone, of course, is free to cavil with my choices, and I freely admit that in certain years I have chosen as much for variety as for significance. As secretary to a congressman or as President of the most powerful nation in the world, Johnson was always inordinately interested in detail. But he never bogged down in specifics, as figuratively he kept his eye on the needs of every sparrow in every nest. One moment he would be talking top policy with his Secretary of State or Secretary of Defense, and a minute later he would be on the telephone to a subordinate 'way down in the chain of command, inquiring about that person's sick child or suggesting a dressmaker or beautician for the man's wife.

What then is important? The fact that Senator Lyndon Johnson helped get the whole space program of the United States underway and was one of the travel agents for the trip to the moon? Or the fact that Congressman Lyndon Johnson hurried up a loan for some corner grocer totally without influence or political clout, so that that man could somehow stay in business and hold his family together?

Or the fact that the kid director of the National Youth Administration in Texas set up NYA programs in that state's black colleges so that some Negro youths in the hopeless Thirties could find a springboard off the farm and out of the menial jobs?

In fact, let's look at the NYA, which usually is disposed of in a few paragraphs in any Johnson biography. Within two months after his appointment in the new agency, Johnson was able to report that 20,000 Texas boys and girls had been placed in schools or given an opportunity to go to work. Of this number, 5,700 had been given part-time jobs in eligible colleges and universities of Texas; approximately 9,000 had been given jobs to help defray incidental expenses in high school; freshman college centers had been opened for 750 high school graduates who did not enter college in the autumn; and 2,000 young men and women from 16 to 25 had been put to work on WPA and NYA projects designed either for adults or exclusively for youths. "The NYA is investing this money in actual, productive work," Johnson said. "It is work which is good for the young people who are doing it, and is of real permanent value . . . ."

Notably, considering the time and place, director Johnson had included three young Negroes in his college program and had established an all-Negro advisory board, which raised some approving eyebrows among young black intellectual activists in Washington like Ralph Bunche and Robert C. Weaver. As Weaver, whom President Johnson later named as the first black Cabinet member, was to say three decades later, Johnson "was shocking some people up on the Hill because he thought that the National Youth Administration ought to go to the poor folks. And it seems as though a lot of nice middle-class people . . . were outraged by this . . . . To make bad matters worse, he was giving a hell of a lot of this money to Mexican-Americans, and Negroes."

Although so-called "Texas brags" have been cheapened by too loud and frequent appearances from the wrong people, the state does possess more than its share of legitimate claims to quality. One role in which Texas led the nation was in turning highway engineering into both a technical and aesthetic pleasure, particularly with its flattening out of highway shoulders, planting native shrubs and wild flowers along rights-of-way, and the creation of roadside parks, which latter now number more than 1100. Even as the nation rushed to embrace the automobile in the 1920's and 1930's, few planners gave thought to the fact that if cars could be driven for longer distances, human needs would need new attention.

Among those who thought early that highways should be designed for pleasure as well as speed was the state director for the NYA, who offered the services of the youth under his direction to the Texas Highway Department to build roadside parks, turnouts for rural mail carriers, and unloading places for school children. The program, begun in the spring of 1936, had already reached 156 parks by the end of the following October. An average of 1934 youths grubbed, cleared, built rock benches, tables, barbecue pits, gravel walks and driveways, and generally beautified parks varying in size from one-half to eight and one-half acres each. As H.A. Ziegler, one of Johnson's assistant district supervisors, reported, "The majority of youths who were afforded employment by the NYA on this highway park gained much knowledge in public works and construction. Since it was the first public job many of them held, they also learned that a man must give an hour's work for an hour's pay."

During the entire year of 1936 the whole highway beautification program for Texas cost the federal government just $34,667.16 for NYA labor and the State of Texas $16,411.68 for supervision, equipment, and material. The NYA director persuaded private owners to donate most of the land. No wonder that the National Deputy Executive Director of the NYA wired his Texas director on the following January 8, 1937: "DESIRE YOU COME TO WASHINGTON FOR INAUGURATION ARRIVING JANUARY 19." The host didn't realize that three months later his guest would be one of his congressional bosses.

So what is the greater service? What belongs and what is omitted? All I know is that for two-fifths of this Twentieth Century Lyndon Baines Johnson provided services for legions of people, both for individuals and for groups as huge as nations. My own desire here is not to analyze, to trumpet successes, nor to criticize errors, but simply to present a sampling panorama of four decades of public service of "honorable favors for honest friends."

                                                                                    J B F

A JOHNSON SAMPLER

Some of the hundreds of acts passed under President Lyndon B. Johnson in his program of hope and opportunity for America

1963
College Facilities
Clean Air
Vocational Education
Indian Vocational Training
Manpower Training

1964
Inter-American Development Bank
Kennedy Cultural Center
Tax Reduction
Presidential Transition
Federal Airport Aid
Farm Program
Chamizal Convention
Pesticide Controls
International Development Association
Civil Rights Act of 1964
Campobello International Park
Urban Mass Transit
Water Resources Research
Federal Highway
Civil Service Pay Raise
War on Poverty
Criminal Justice
Truth-in-Securities
Medicine Bow National Forest
Ozark Scenic Riverway
Administrative Conference
Fort Bowie Historic Site
Food Stamp
Housing Act
Interest Equalization
Wilderness Areas
Nurse Training
Revenues for Recreation
Fire Island National Seashore
Library Services
Federal Employee Health Benefits

1965
Medicare
Aid to Education
Higher Education
Four Year Farm Program
Department of Housing and Urban Development
Housing Act
Social Security Increase
Voting Rights
Fair Immigration Law
Older Americans
Heart, Cancer, Stroke Program

Law Enforcement Assistance
National Crime Commission
Drug Controls
Mental Health Facilities
Health Professions
Medical Libraries
Vocational Rehabilitation
Anti-Poverty Program
Arts and Humanities Foundation
Aid to Appalachia
Highway Beauty
Clean Air
Water Pollution Control
High Speed Transit
Manpower Training
Presidential Disability
Child Health
Regional Development
Aid to Small Businesses
Weather-Predicting Services
Military Pay Increase
GI Life Insurance
Community Health Services
Water Resources Council
Water Desalting
Assateague National Seashore
Whiskeytown National Recreation Area
Delaware Water Gap Recreation Area
Juvenile Delinquency Control
Arms Control
Strengthening U.N. Charter
International Coffee Agreement
Retirement for Public Servants

1966
Food for India
Child Nutrition
Department of Transportation
Truth in Packaging
Model Cities
Rent Supplements
Teachers Corps
Asian Development Bank
Clean Rivers
Food for Freedom
Child Safety
Narcotics Rehabilitation

Traffic Safety
Highway Safety
Mine Safety
International Education
Bail Reform
Tire Safety
New GI Bill
Minimum Wage Increase
Urban Mass Transit
Civil Procedure Reform
Federal Highway Aid
Military Medicare
Public Health Reorganization
Cape Lookout Seashore
Water Research
Guadalupe National Park
Revolutionary War Bicentennial
Fish-Wildlife Preservation
Water for Peace
Anti-Inflation Program
Scientific Knowledge Exchange
Cultural Materials Exchange
Foreign Investors Tax
Parcel Post Reform
Civil Service Pay Raise
Stockpile Sales
Participation Certificates
Protection for Savings
Flexible Interest Rates
Freedom of Information

1967
Education Professions
Education Act
Air Pollution Control
Partnership for Health
Social Security Increases
Age Discrimination
Wholesome Meat
Flammable Fabrics
Urban Research
Public Broadcasting
Outer Space Treaty
Modern D.C. Government
Vietnam Veterans Benefits
Federal Judicial Center
Civilian-Postal Workers Pay
Deaf-Blind Center
College Work Study
Summer Youth Programs
Food Stamps
Rail Strike Settlement
Selective Service
Urban Fellowships
Consular Treaty
Safety At Sea Treaty
Narcotics Treaty
Anti-Racketeering
Product Safety Commission
Small Business Aid
Inter-American Bank

1968
Fair Housing
Indian Bill of Rights
Safe Streets
Wholesome Poultry
Food for Peace
Commodity Exchange Rules
U.S. Grain Standards
School Breakfasts
Bank Protection
Defense Production
Corporate Takeovers
Export Program
Gold Cover Removal
Truth-in-Lending
Aircraft Noise Abatement
Auto Insurance Study
New Narcotics Bureau
Gas Pipeline Safety
Fire Safety
Sea Grant Colleges
D.C. School Board
Tax Surcharge
Better Housing
International Monetary Reform
International Grains Treaty
Oil Revenues for Recreation
Virgin Islands Elections
San Rafael Wilderness
San Gabriel Wilderness
Fair Federal Juries
Candidate Protection
Juvenile Delinquency Prevention
Guaranteed Student Loans
D.C. Visitors Center
FHA-VA Interest Rate Programs
Health Manpower
Eisenhower College
Gun Controls
Aid-to-Handicapped Children
Redwoods Park
Flaming Gorge Recreation Area
Biscayne Park
Heart, Cancer and Stroke Programs
Hazardous Radiation Protection
Colorado River Reclamation
Scenic Rivers
Scenic Trails
National Water Commission
Federal Magistrates
Vocational Education
Veterans Pension Increases
North Cascades Park
International Coffee Agreement
Intergovernmental Manpower
Dangerous Drugs Control
Military Justice Code

A trip anywhere with Lyndon Baines Johnson was a frantic experience, whether to a ball game or on a foreign visit of state. On one such trip to Asia, everyone except the President had run himself into a state of exhaustion when George Christian, his press secretary, "then 40 going on 80," remarked quietly to several reporters:

"When he's gone, you guys are going to miss him."

36TH PRESIDENT OF THE UNITED STATES

From the official portrait that hangs in The White House,
by Madame Elizabeth Shoumatoff.

Lady Bird Johnson

From the official portrait that hangs in The White House,
by Madame Elizabeth Shoumatoff.

NOVEMBER 1972
AT THE LBJ RANCH

BIRTHPLACE
STONEWALL, TEXAS

BOYHOOD HOME
JOHNSON CITY, TEXAS

RESIDENCE
LBJ RANCH

LBJ CENTER

William W. Heath began his professional career as a piney woods county attorney in East Texas. Step by step he moved up the political ladder, until when he died he was known as Mr. Ambassador for his ministry to Sweden and as the former chairman of the Board of Regents of The University of Texas. It was under his chairmanship that the University made its dignified transition from a lily-white school to an integrated university, an act which he often described as the proudest accomplishment of his life.

If that proud accomplishment had not occurred, Heath undoubtedly would have pointed to the creation of the Lyndon Baines Johnson Presidential Library and the Lyndon B. Johnson School of Public Affairs as his proudest accomplishments, but in his scale of values he placed human advance ahead of even scholarly advance. While he was chairman and while Johnson was President, Heath and his chancellor, Harry Huntt Ransom, began hard thinking about bringing the projected Library to the University campus. They knew of the arguments against them. Pressures existed to place the Library elsewhere. The University of Texas constituency, from the Regents through the faculty and students and on to the Texas political apparatus and the citizenry itself, were badly split over the Johnson Administration. With as many social advances as Johnson was espousing, as well as the problems with Vietnam and Santo Domingo, it invariably touched someone's raw nerve exposed to change or involvement.

But Heath and Ransom persevered. They found a strong ally in Lady Bird Johnson, herself an alumna of the University. When the two daughters, Lynda and Luci, later attended the University, they augmented the campaign for the Library to be placed at The University of Texas.

The argument that apparently sold Johnson on the University was that unlike all previous Presidential libraries, such a facility actually belonged at a University where for generations to come scholars interested in government, history, economics, law, the making of law, education, civil rights, space, and a host of other inquiries would gather from all over the world to research and write. As Heath later said simply, "And he bought that argument."

Once the Library was placed, Heath and Mrs. Johnson visited Presidential and university libraries to see what they were doing well and where their disappointments lay. Along the way they became convinced that one deficiency of libraries wrapped around the careers of famous people was in their under-use. As Heath said of one, "it's like being in a mausoleum—there's just not anybody in there . . . ." An idea began to form—why not build a school around the LBJ Library where scholars could profit from the papers therein and could utilize them toward present and future problem solving? On this concept the President needed no selling.

The result is the Library and the School of Public Affairs. The University of Texas built the two structures, and then leased the Library space in perpetuity to The National Archives as a branch of the General Services Administration. It is the first Presidential library on a university campus. The John F. Kennedy Library, now in temporary quarters, is being built on the Harvard University campus, and indications are that one of the California campuses will be chosen for the Richard

M.Nixon Library. The Johnson Library therefore may be the start of something new and continuing, so that future Presidential libraries may be placed at some crossroads of scholarship rather than at the accidental locale where a future President was born or grew up.

Like Johnson himself, the Library has evoked strong feelings. It stands on a rolling greensward, cornered by several motts of trees, notably spreading liveoaks. Its principal architect, Gordon Bunshaft of Skidmore, Owings and Merrill, designed it the way he saw Lyndon B. Johnson—massive, and overpowering its surroundings. No one ignores the structure.

Inside, the influence of both the President and Mrs. Johnson may be seen. President Harry S. Truman purportedly told President Johnson that the reproduction of the White House Oval Office was the most popular public portion of his own library, and advised President Johnson that he should incorporate it into his structure. Johnson agreed. For her part, Mrs. Johnson had observed that most casual visitors saw exhibits but had no true perception that actual work with manuscripts and books went on behind a library's scene. She therefore wanted a segment of the President's files somehow displayed, and so several stories of red library cartons can be seen through the windows fronting on the Great Hall.

Here then came the great and the loyal for the dedication on May 21, 1971. Here President Richard M. Nixon became the first signer of the guest book at the reception desk. He saw a first floor displaying gifts of heads of state, huge pictures of the interior of the White House and the wedding gowns of Lynda and Luci, as well as simple letters from such diverse people as Robert F. Kennedy and Pope John XXIII. He may also have seen a large case of such presents from ordinary people as a horse's head outlined in Victorian, mostly black buttons, a patchwork quilt from samples obtained from the wives of all the governors, an embroidered Presidential seal, a French army bugle of World War I, and a Persian Kashan rug featuring the American eagle holding the American flag. The second floor represents the serious and the carnival sides of politics—from campaign posters from James A. Garfield to recordings of Franklin D. Roosevelt's Fireside Chats. One section is even devoted to a panoply of losers. To some viewers' surprise, another large panel displays letters critical of the policy in Vietnam.

Next door is a three-story building "as long as three football fields," as some newsmen like to point out. Here is housed the Lyndon B. Johnson School of Public Affairs, which represents not only the thirty-seven years of public service depicted here, but the extra six years in which Johnson practiced good works without official benefit of public office. Under the guidance of its first dean, John Gronouski, himself a cabinet officer under Kennedy and Johnson and the first Polish-speaking ambassador ever to Poland, the school has broken ground in its preparation of young people for that most frequently sought but educationally neglected career, the service of the public at local, state, national and international levels.

Through these two agencies, not to mention the myriad of other achievements, Lyndon B. Johnson will continue to serve the public in the generations ahead.

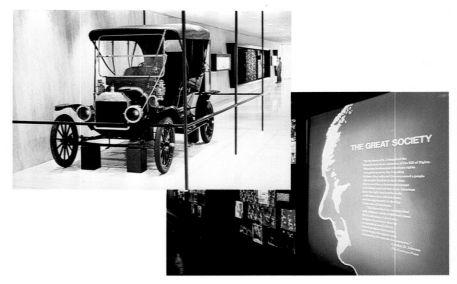

A WORD ABOUT THE TEXT

The items in this book have obviously come from a variety of sources. Some are taken from the speeches and news releases of Lyndon Johnson that reside in the Presidential Library. Newspaper excerpts have usually been identified. In general, the newspapers ranged from Los Angeles to New York, with a natural preponderance of excerpts from Texas papers. The opening and closing quotations are from an article by Hugh Sidey in *Life*, April 24, 1970. The *Public Papers of the Presidents* from Harry S. Truman through Lyndon B. Johnson have also supplied documents. The title pages of acts have come from the Johnson Library. *The Congressional Record* and *Congress and the Nation* have also been consulted.

Since nothing like this is ever completed without the generosity and help of others, I must acknowledge debt to several people. I have leaned most heavily on Michael Gillette of the Johnson Library staff, but the other members of that staff, notably Charles Corkran and Frank Wolfe, have unfailingly come up with what I needed. Luther Thompson of the Steck-Warlick Company has been my constant adviser and pusher. At The University of Texas, J. C. Martin and Robert Martin of the Texas Newspaper Collection have chased down my vague remembrances of dates and articles. And as is becoming habitual and automatic in my endeavors, my family helped by postponing their own projects, and Colleen Kain and Ruth Mathews put it all together.

The letter from Robert S. Allen and the excerpts from the article by Horace Busby are being used with permission from the respective authors.

Joe B. Frantz

THE 1ST YEAR – 1931

Fredericksburg, Texas, lies 31 miles west of Johnson City, with Stonewall, the birthplace of Lyndon B. Johnson, half-way between. In that sparsely settled area people keep up with each other, and so in 1931 the editor of the Fredericksburg *Standard* felt his readers would be interested in a two-paragraph story about the new position of the son of a former legislator. His headline is memorable for its simplicity, and for what, in retrospect, it portends. Much more space in the *Standard* was devoted that month to the news that Reno had just totted up its divorces during the first six months of its new easy residence law and found that more than 3,000 divorces had already been issued. And Handy Andy grocery was selling winesap apples for 25 cents for two dozen. No one realized that the resignation of a Houston teacher meant that a career that would help shape America and the world had now begun.

Teacher Named Kleberg's Aide

San Marcos, Tex., Nov. 29 -- Lyndon Baines Johnson, 23, whose family resides here and who was graduted from the Southwest Texas State Teachers' College of San Marcos, has been appointed private secretary to Congressman-elect R. M. Kleberg of Corpus Christi, according to news received here today.

Johnson is the son of Sam Johnson, former member of the Legislature and now chief investigator for the State Railroad Commission He has been teaching the last year in the department of public speaking in Sam Houston High School, Houston. He is a native of Johnson City.

THE 2ND YEAR – 1932

Congressman Richard M. Kleberg was, in one observer's words, "a bluff and good natured multi-millionaire who . . . had no particular interest in being a congressman except for the prestige . . . and spent some time looking after cattle legislation pending before the House Committee on Agriculture." An excellent Spanish scholar, he loved to write his innumerable contacts in Mexico, which reputedly annoyed his pragmatic young secretary, since the recipients were not constituents. Meanwhile Gene Latimer, a member of the Sam Houston High School (Houston, Texas) debate team which under Coach Lyndon Johnson had won every contest it entered except the state final, joined his former teacher in Washington. Secretary Johnson installed him as a roommate in the basement of the Dodge Hotel and put him to work writing the Congressman's letters. Although the only course that Latimer had ever flunked in high school was in typing, Johnson decided to become the youngster's new typing instructor, and under his stern, around-the-clock tutelage Latimer could type 85 words a minute with few errors within two months after his arrival in Washington. The material on the facing pace is taken from the transcript of Latimer's taped oral recollections about that first year.

. . . By the time I arrived the Chief had ["know-how"] in abundance, including how to get such jobs at the Capitol as elevator operator, post office employee, House doorkeeper for the gallery, etc. In some offices these jobs went to relatives or sons of the members' close friends, and after the job was over (and the hours were not long) the employee was at leisure.

The Chief had a slightly different concept. In order to handle the amount of correspondence his fertile brain decided was requisite to keeping up strong political fences in the district, more office help was needed than the regular office appropriation would permit. So after performance of the duties of whatever patronage job one might have as a result of Mr. Kleberg's House membership, it was understood that the employee then reported for his real job to the Chief. Therefore, although I had a prize patronage job with the House post office, in between mail deliveries and after the last one, I was engaged in seeing how many letters I could get out for Mr. Kleberg's signature, executed and approved by Mr. Johnson.

. . . it was evident the congressman reposed complete confidence in his secretary to run his office and to make suggestions for his well-being both political and otherwise. In short, the Chief was the congressman from the Texas 14th district in all but name.

I recall that contrary to most office arrangements the Chief had his desk immediately inside the entrance door, so that one coming in could not possibly advance further without his interception. And here the congressman's business was run, except when a good friend or an important person called. The Chief would steer him into Mr. Kleberg's private office for discussion. Here at the entrance too, was where he weeded out the casual visitor who just "happened to be in town," talked with him 30 seconds, and had him out of the office and on his way in another 30, happily clutching an autographed photo of the congressman and passes to the House and Senate galleries. All the while the typewriters never lost a beat.

THE 3RD YEAR – 1933

Political pundits who claim the power to foresee should have been alerted that a new force had entered the Washington arena when on a Tuesday night in April a group of "liberals" startled a complacent "Little Congress" by throwing precedent to the winds and electing Lyndon Johnson, secretary to Congressman Kleberg of Texas and a virtual newcomer to the Capitol, as its speaker. As a result, the 24-year-old received his first interview in a Washington newspaper, a two-column article complete with photograph. Although unsigned, it was written by Gould Lincoln, who would cover the Johnson story as the new "speaker" advanced from Congressman to President over the next three decades.

Little Congress Upset
PROGRESSIVES PUT OVER NEW SLATE IN ELECTION DRIVE.

PROGRESSIVE secretaries of House members and Senators have overridden a precedent of 14 years in the election of officers of the Little Congress—the secretarial organization modeled after Congress. More than 250 persons attended the session Tuesday night, which was the most lively in the history of that organization, one of the founders of which was Kenneth Romney, now sergeant at arms of the House.

In open revolt against the conduct of "the Little Congress" by an "oligarchy" of veteran members, the insurgents smashed a rule that the speaker of the Little Congress be drafted from the clerkship, and that the sergeant at arms be made clerk. The "liberals," composed principally of Democrats and two Farmer-Laborites, voted in an entirely new slate of officers, choosing Lyndon Johnson, secretary to Representative Kleberg of Texas, as their titular head.

Using campaign tactics followed by the members of Congress, the liberals branded the former office holders as "standpatters," "obstructionists," "dictatorial" and "reactionary" in their control of the Little Congress. The result climaxed a secret campaign with Liberal leaders holding executive conferences, followed by a systematic door-to-door canvass of the House and Senate Office Buildings the night before the election.

The scalding remarks of Grady C. Durham of Louisiana, Robert Lee Smith of New York and Aaron M. Litman of Minnesota in nominating the progressive slate, rivaled many of the "remarks" made in the House itself, which were subsequently stricken from the permanent record. In addition to the election of Mr. Johnson as speaker, the slate that won included: Jack Frost, secretary to Representative John Wood of Georgia, as clerk and Ray Johnson (Farmer-Laborite), secretary to Representative Henry Arens of Minnesota, as sergeant at arms.

Pledging a "new deal," and to be mindful of "the forgotten man," in accepting the office of speaker, Mr. Johnson stated: "I mean that my election tonight will mark just such a new deal for all Little Congresses, and by that I mean that every one regardless of party affiliations will receive square treatment from the chair. Committees will be named on an equitable basis of membership and seniority."

THE 4TH YEAR – 1934

In September Johnson made a quick trip to Austin, where he met a recent graduate of The University of Texas, Miss Claudia Alta Taylor. In his usual tornadic irresistible style Johnson "campaigned" for the young lady's hand, and two months later, on November 17, 1934, Lyndon Baines Johnson and Lady Bird Johnson were married in San Antonio. Many long-time Lyndon Johnson-watchers maintain that his bringing Lady Bird into public view was the greatest service he ever performed for either the nation or for himself, that she provided the perfect balance wheel to give his whirlwind energies direction, and that she has given the nation a sense of its own beauty and quality that is unmatched. A sometime Johnson critic like Senator Ralph Yarborough has paid tribute to "her mind and soul" and the fact that "'Lady Bird' has been at his side in every contest." And Senator Herman Talmadge has asserted that she "is not only gracious and charming, but has rare perception and insight." Laurance Rockefeller, who has worked with her on many a project, perhaps sums up best a portion of her strength and her contribution. She is, he says, "so self-transcendent that it [is] amazing . . . a real professional person in the right sense of the word . . . she works hard to achieve great results. She knows it means discipline . . . . I'm always awed by the way she focuses her attention and her conversation and her efforts on things that she considers top priority and refuses to be diverted . . . ."

Marriages

JOHNSON-TAYLOR.

Friends in Marshall and Karnack will be interested in the announcement of the marriage of Miss Claudia Taylor of Karnack to Lyndon Johnson, which took place Saturday afternoon, November 17, at St. Mark's Episcopal Church in San Antonio, Texas.

The bride, who is known to her friends as "Lady Bird" Taylor, is the daughter of T. J. Taylor and the late Mrs. Minnie Lee Patillo Taylor of Karnack. She was graduated from the Marshall High School and St. Mary's College in Dallas, and received her B. A. and B. J. degrees from the State University at Austin.

Mr. Johnson, whose home is in Corpus Christi, is secretary to United States Congressman Kleberg and is speaker of Little Congress. He holds an LL. D. degree.

After a wedding trip to Monterrey and Mexico City, Mr. and Mrs. Johnson will make their home in Washington, D. C.

THE 5TH YEAR – 1935

He had, as the recent popular song suggests, "only just begun" when in the summer of 1935 he became State Director of the National Youth Administration for Texas. Typically he came out of the new starting gate with all the quick acceleration of a racing thoroughbred. He had a new job, he foresaw new opportunities, and he felt the need to get rolling. Although Aubrey Williams, the National Director, was a man of status and Johnson a 27-year-old beginner, in his very first letter the Texan was urging his chief to join him in getting going. Like Stephen Vincent Benét's Americans, he was "always moving on," and he swept along superiors, colleagues, and subordinates in his restless, usually irresistible tide.

NATIONAL YOUTH ADMINISTRATION
604 Littlefield Building
Austin, Texas

August 8, 1935

Honorable Aubrey Williams
Director of the National Youth Administration
Johnson-Walker Building
Washington, D.C.

Dear Mr. Williams:

We have a big state, consequently a big job; and since our time is short, if we are going to put the program over, we must start moving. Won't you have the proper authority go into the attached report from every angle and let me have a decision at the earliest possible date. I am in hopes we can know something definite about this plan before the state directors' meeting in Washington later in the month.

Sincerely,

Lyndon B. Johnson,
NYA Director for Texas

LBJ LJ
encl.

THE 6TH YEAR – 1936

The National Youth Administration produced no hoe-leaners or shovel soldiers, as was charged against some of the other New Deal agencies—at least not in Texas. By the end of October 1936 Johnson could point out that 54,117 hours had been spent in building recreation facilities; 56,885 books had been repaired in libraries; 487,451 hours had been devoted to public service projects; 108,208 garments had been sewed for the poor; 11,637 hours had been assigned to research; and 48,010 hours of assistance covering 136,030 acres had been given to county agents and county home demonstration agents. In addition the needy youth of Texas had prepared 163,753 school lunches for even more needy, had canned seven and a half tons of food, had laid 12 miles of sidewalks, had spent 5,064 hours in nurseries, and had surveyed 574 acres of park land. Particularly they had beautified Texas in a way that had always made that state deservedly outstanding for the convenience and pleasure of its highways. One hundred and fifty-six roadside parks, the first in the United States, had been created, and plants and other improvements had been set alongside 874 miles of highway. Obviously, the National Youth Administration was at work in Texas.

January 23, 1936

Honorable Richard R. Brown
Assistant Executive Director NYA
1734 New York Avenue, NW
Washington, D.C.

<u>Attention: Miss Helen Herrmann</u>

Dear Miss Herrman:

I have just received your letter of January 20. You now have the complete picture of the Texas camps, including expenditures, personnel, administration, activities, etc.

We now realize that we had the enthusiasm that only youth has when we asked for three camps. These camps brought us headaches of all kinds; we worked day and night with them. We had to secure the active cooperation and participation of everyone from the Governor of the State to the poorest paid Case Worker to make them what they were. We have placed in employment more than ninety per cent of all the girls that we had in our three camps.

I would surely appreciate your reading the Texas camp reports carefully, studying their contents, and making some suggestions that we might well have used to improve our camps in any detail. These suggestions would prove valuable to us in getting our camps underway next season.

I hope you or Miss Smith will be able to come to Texas sometime within the not too distant future and outline a new procedure to us with which we can begin our camps in March, or soon after.

With every good wish, I am

Sincerely yours,

Lyndon B. Johnson
NYA Director for Texas

LBJ LJE

THE 7TH YEAR – 1937

In early spring of 1937 Lyndon Johnson resigned as State Director of the NYA to run for the unexpired term of the late Congressman James P. Buchanan of Texas' Tenth District. Although in Texas considerable disenchantment had set in with the New Deal for various reasons, Johnson shrewdly surmised that Franklin D. Roosevelt had enough supporters that in a race of ten candidates he could win with a forthright 100 percent New Deal campaign. The result was that on April 10, 1937 Lyndon B. Johnson took his seat in Congress for an elected public service career that would cover 11,608 days before it terminated on Inauguration Day 1969. During his campaign he had promised aggressive representation, and had told all the things he would do if elected. In his case campaign promises proved to be more than just political rhetoric, as the Brenham *Banner Press* reported when on his return from his freshman session Johnson made his first speech to that heavily German-Polish town. In greater detail than reported here, Johnson analyzed each of his pledges, ending each one with the solemn and fervid proclamation: "That job has been done." Significantly the new Congressman closed with another pledge—to visit and report regularly. "But," he added, "my job is a twelve-months job, and I do not need any layoffs."

In his address, following an introduction by Mayor Reese B. Lockett, the congressman reviewed his pledge made during the campaign last spring to complete Marshall Ford dam near Austin; push the Brazos river flood control plan; assist farm tenants to own their own farms; increase farm income; and obtain farm relief. All of these jobs have been done, he said, with the exception of the farm bill which is scheduled first on the calendar at the next meeting of congress.

Regarding proposed crop control legislation, he said that he hoped to see scientific laboratories established to find new uses and wider markets for cotton; but that until distribution catches up with production, the latter must be controlled or the farmer will face ruin.

Defends Hour-Wage Bill

He deviated from his prepared speech to put in a good word for the hours and wages bill which he said would eliminate abuses existing in industry.

Replying to the criticism that the bill if passed would prevent industries from moving into the south, he asserted: "If an industry cannot pay decent wages, I do not want it in my district."

THE 8TH YEAR – 1938

On August 27, 1966, President Johnson did a little birthday reminiscing. Among other things, he told how David Dubinsky, former president of the International Ladies Garment Workers Union, persuaded three Texas Congressmen to sign a petition to call a Democratic party caucus preliminary to pushing through the first minimum wage law in the United States—for 25 cents an hour. Nowadays after thirty-five years of minimum wage laws only the most rigid reject the idea, but in 1938 the idea was anathema to a large portion of the population, especially in the South and in Texas. As Johnson recalled, "we were all threatened with political oblivion and defeat. Two of [the three Texans who supported the petition] were defeated in the next election . . . —Maury Maverick of San Antonio and Congressman [W.D.] McFarlane of Wichita Falls . . . . I don't know what happened to me except I didn't have an opponent." Although the three Congressmen were saluted by labor and by the progressive press in the United States for their courage in the face of almost certain defeat, only Johnson survived to enjoy the praise for the bravery. It remained one of his proudest votes as a Congressman.

MOTION TO DISCHARGE COMMITTEE

MAY 6, 1938.

TO THE CLERK OF THE HOUSE OF REPRESENTATIVES:

Pursuant to clause 4 of rule XXVII, I, Hon. MARY T. NORTON, move to discharge the Committee on Rules from the consideration of the resolution (H. Res. 478) entitled "A resolution making S. 2475 a special order of business," which was referred to said committee April 26, 1938, in support of which motion the undersigned Members of the House of Representatives affix their signatures, to wit:

85. Frank J. G. Dorsey.
86. John Kee.
87. Jennings Randolph.
88. Joe L. Smith.
89. Robert L. Ramsay.
90. George W. Johnson.
91. Charles I. Faddis.
92. Ed. V. Izac.
93. Byron N. Scott.
94. H. K. Claypool.
95. Frank W. Fries.
96. Edith Nourse Rogers.
97. Merlin Hull.
98. J. Joseph Smith.
99. M. A. Romjue.
100. Patrick J. Boland.
101. Joseph Gray.
102. J. B. Shannon.
103. Knute Hill.
104. C. Arthur Anderson.
105. Jas. M. Mead.
106. Donald L. O'Toole.
107. Edward W. Patterson.
108. W. H. Larrabee.
109. Henry G. Teigan.
110. John J. Cochran.
111. Andrew L. Somers.
112. Don Gingery.
113. Harry L. Haines.
114. Wm. Lemke.
115. Fred Biermann.
116. Phil Ferguson.
117. Andrew J. Transue.
118. John Luecke.
119. Arthur W. Mitchell.
120. Martin J. Kennedy.
121. Compton I. White.
122. Gomer Smith.
123. W. D. McFarlane.
159. Maury Maverick.
160. George D. O'Brien.
161. Arthur W. Aleshire.
162. Adolph Sabath.
163. Edward L. O'Neill.
164. Herman L. Eberharter.
165. Frank Crowther.
166. J. Buell Snyder.
167. John J. Boylan.
168. Thomas R. Amlie.
169. R. E. Thomason.
170. D. Lane Powers.
171. Joseph W. Martin, Jr.
172. John F. Dockweiler.
173. Lyndon B. Johnson.
174. Melvin J. Maas.
175. Harry L. Englebright.
176. John M. Houston.
177. John A. Martin.
178. Albert E. Carter.
179. Louis Ludlow.
180. George G. Sadowski.
181. Everett Dirksen.
182. William I. Sirovich.
183. Sam Massingale.
184. Glenn Griswold.
185. Hugh M. Rigney.
186. R. B. Wigglesworth.
187. James C. Oliver.
188. Charles R. Clason.
189. Leonard W. Schuetz.
190. George J. Bates.
191. Arthur B. Jenks.
192. Emanuel Celler.
193. James P. McGranery.
194. Walter M. Pierce.
195. Chester Thompson.
196. Harold G. Mosier.
197. Jack Nichols.

THE 9TH YEAR – 1939

In 1939 the writer drove after dark from Galveston to Austin, approximately 225 miles, for the first time. He thought this must be the loneliest, most isolated area he'd ever been through, for aside from the small towns he did not see more than three or four lights along the entire route. As he learned later, people were there, but the electricity wasn't. Such a dearth of power was not unique with Texas but infested farmers throughout the nation, making them truly second-class occupationally. One of Johnson's early projects was to bring rural electrification to his district. As a freshman Congressman pushing through a major electric cooperative project, he showed that skill to work with the opposition which would prove such a hallmark of his political career, especially during the days as Senate Majority Leader. As Benjamin Reed Cohen said in a memo to President Roosevelt, Johnson "has done an admirable job in working out the problems of Texas' little TVA."Johnson, in Cohen's words, had proved "cooperation between public and private power is not impossible as Willkie claims."

LYNDON B. JOHNSON
10TH TEXAS DISTRICT

Congress of the United States
House of Representatives
Washington, D. C.

July the eighteenth
1 9 3 9

My dear Mr. President:

As you know, I have been following closely the
progress of the Lower Colorado River Authority, the Texas
flood control and power project which has been financed by
the P. W. A.

I want to call your attention the recent developments in the affairs of the Authority. Preparations have
been almost completed by the Authority to take over the Texas
Power and Light Company properties in a sixteen-county area
adjoining the Authority's hydro generating plants.

Because the consumption of the electricity in the
area acquired by the Authority is not sufficient at the present time to afford a market for all the electricity which will
be generated at the Authority's four dams, a contract has been
entered into for the sale of part of the Authority's surplus
power to the Texas Power and Light Company. Under the terms
of this contract, the Authority will be assured of the sale
of a large block of surplus power and yet will retain the privilege of recapturing it to supply municipal and public agencies
when more power is needed for that purpose. The power company
has also agreed to pass on to the public any savings that accrue
from the purchase of this power.

I want you to know that the Lower Colorado River
Authority is making this progress in its public service and
that it has received the cooperation of one of the local
private utilities in the area.

With assurances of my great esteem, believe me,

Sincerely

Lyndon B. Johnson

THE 10TH YEAR – 1940

In the mid-term elections of 1938 the Democrats lost eighty-two seats in Congress. With Roosevelt running for an unprecedented and controversial third term and with the natural disaffection that various individuals and groups develop for any party in power over a protracted period, the Democrats were truly worried that they might lose both the Presidency to Wendell Willkie and control of Congress to the Republicans in 1940. Late in the campaign, on advice of official men like Congressman Sam Rayburn and more private men like James Rowe, Sr., the President and Democratic hierarchy decided to entrust the chores of fund-raising and obtaining votes for Congressmen in danger to 32-year-old Lyndon B. Johnson. With less than two effective months to help his fellow Democrats return to Congress, Johnson pitched in with characteristic energy and organization, particularly in the Middle West, where the Democrats feared losing twelve seats in Illinois, five in Indiana, and three in Missouri. As Robert S. Allen, columnist, wrote after the election, Johnson performed a miracle, but only after Johnson had written the President on October 1, "The present forty-five margin gives me the night-sweats at three a.m."

C O P Y

November 7, 1940

Honorable Sam Rayburn
Speaker of the House
House Office Building
Washington, D. C.

Dear Sam:

Now that the campaign is over and we are all celebrating, I would like to inject a serious note for a minute with a few observations about the future.

In the final couple weeks of the fight I had an opportunity to watch at close range what in my opinion was one of the most effective campaign efforts I have ever seen. I am referring to the work that was done by Lyndon Johnson in the congressional field. I am sure I don't have to tell you about Lyndon and what a grand and able youngster he is. He's got everything a good public official should have: He's got an enlightened view, he's got courage, drive, ability and, above all, loyalty--loyalty to his friends and to the principles he believes in.

His work in the campaign, in my opinion, was one of the few really good jobs done in the campaign. . . .

Lyndon performed miracles . . . .

(Robert S. Allen)

THE 11TH YEAR – 1941

The summer and autumn of 1941 seemed to stretch out interminably. France had fallen to Hitler's *blitzkrieg* more than a year before, and Hitler's armies were overrunning the Western plains of Russia, knocking at the very doors of Moscow itself. England stood alone, as it had for a year. In the United States men argued whether the draft law should be extended, and the Great Debate reached its peak on whether the United States owed it to civilization to help stop the march of fascism and militarism by Germany, Italy, and Japan. The House of Representatives agreed to extend the draft by just one vote—one vote alone kept the United States from having no draft army on Pearl Harbor day. In Texas Lyndon Johnson was running, primarily against former Governor W. Lee "Pappy" O'Daniel, for the Senate seat vacated through the death of Morris Sheppard. After seeming to be a sure winner when the first day of returns was completed, Johnson saw a disproportionate number of the last 4,000 votes in late reporting boxes go to O'Daniel, so that Johnson lost by a bare 1,000-vote margin. Back in Congress, Johnson declared for President Roosevelt by giving his vote to draft extension and in other ways voting for assistance to England and for American preparedness. During his campaign for the Senate he had taken notice of the lowering war clouds and had pledged to young voters and their sweethearts and mothers that he would not send their sons anywhere he would not go himself. Immediately after Congress voted to declare that a state of war existed between the United States and the Axis powers, Congressman Johnson became the first member of either House to go on active duty—in Johnson's case, with the Navy, in which he held a reserve commission.

My hope as your Senator is that I shall never have to vote to send your boy to the trenches. But I say to you mothers: The day my conscience tells me to vote that way, 32-year-old Lyndon Johnson, who registered in the draft, will give up his Senate seat to go with your boy.

THE 12TH YEAR – 1942

On June 9 Johnson rode a B-26 as an observer on a bombing raid over the Japanese base at Lae in New Guinea. Just as his plane was approaching the target, it developed trouble in one engine, so that it fell behind its group. For sometime thereafter the B-26, jettisoning bombs as fast as it could, played tag with Japanese Zeroes, which could maneuver about 100 miles an hour faster. The rolling threw Johnson all over the radio compartment, but eventually, after one certain kill, the plane limped in barely above ocean level to the Australian base at Port Moresby. After General Douglas MacArthur had chided Johnson gently for risking his life and Johnson had replied that he knew of no other way to give the President and his constituents a personal report, General MacArthur awarded him the Silver Star, explaining that in Melbourne he had neither Silver Stars nor citations, but that both would be forthcoming. When the citation did arrive, it was awarded "For gallantry in action . . . . Lieutenant Commander Johnson, in order to obtain personal knowledge of combat conditions, volunteered as an observer on a hazardous aerial combat mission over hostile positions in New Guinea [and] evidenced marked coolness in spite of the hazard involved. His gallant action enabled him to obtain and return with valuable information."

In mid-summer, 1942, Lieutenant Commander Johnson, like all the other Congressmen who had gone on active duty with the armed services, had resumed his seat at the request of President Roosevelt. He was named chairman of a subcommittee for the Naval Affairs Committee for special investigation into navy procurement methods and management of its war efforts.

REP. JOHNSON SEES AIRMEN IN ACTION

Texan in Australia Starts Out on Bombing Mission but Plane Has to Return

---

HE PRAISES OUR TROOPS

Close Friend of President Says There Is Nothing Wrong With ~~Them~~—'They Are Americans'

By BYRON DARNTON
Wireless to THE NEW YORK TIMES.

AT UNITED NATIONS OPER-ATIONAL BASE in Southwest Pacific, June 10 (Delayed)—Representative Lyndon Johnson of Texas, who is a Lieutenant Commander in the naval reserve and a close friend of President Roosevelt, paid a visit here yesterday and took off on a bombing mission for Lae, New Guinea.

The plane, piloted by Lieutenant Walter Greer of Russellville, Ark., developed mechanical trouble and was forced to return without reaching its target. But the Representative got a good first-hand idea of the troubles and problems confronting our airmen and declared himself greatly impressed by the skill and courage of the bomber crews and fighter pilots.

"There is nothing wrong with these youths," he said. "They are real Americans with real American courage."

THE 13TH YEAR – 1943

No champion, whether he be artist, athlete, or politician, wins every time, and Lyndon Johnson proved to be no exception. But whether the issue involved principle, as in his several speeches to Congress during this year against absenteeism in America's war industries; or whether the problem looked to the local needs of his constituents, Congressman Johnson threw himself into each contest as if it were the most important event in his political life—as it probably was, at that moment. But in trying to get a V-12 unit placed at Texas College of Arts and Industries, Johnson ran into an immovable object, probably because, as Rear Admiral Randall Jacobs, USN, wrote him, "Texas . . . already has an unusually high number of commitments [from the Navy]." But undoubtedly Johnson was speaking precisely when he wrote his old friend, Sam Fore. He never surrendered gracefully until he had indeed "argued, cajoled, threatened, and begged."

May the third
1 9 4 3

Honorable Sam Fore, Jr.
Floresville, Texas

Dear Sam;

I've argued, cajoled, threatened and begged, but
am about at the end of my rope on the inclusion of Texas
College of Arts and Industries in the Navy College Training Program under V-12 at this time.

Navy quotas are nearly complete in all fields, and
particularly is this true in Texas where the Navy has
already made an unusual number of commitments.

I'm always disappointed when I can't bring you
some good news, but I guess we can't expect to bat 1,000
per cent all the time.

Affectionate regards from

Your amigo

Lyndon B. Johnson

gl
war projects
a & i, kingsville

THE 14TH YEAR – 1944

In the 77th, 78th, and 79th Congresses Lyndon Johnson served on the House Naval Affairs Committee, as chairman of the Aeronautics and Ordnance subcommittees, as chairman of a Special Subcommittee on Personnel, and on eighteen other subcommittees dealing with naval affairs. By now, in his mid-thirties, he was being recognized as one of the most capable Congressmen, whose interests and accomplishments carried him far beyond his specific Congressional assignments and whose constituency ranged outside his own Tenth District into all of Texas, plus a considerable portion of the remainder of the nation. Thus it is no surprise to see him surface as the spokesman for the poultrymen of the nation in their efforts to obtain a fair share of the ultimate value of their produce. Notably, most of Texas' metropolitan newspapers, which did not care for federal distribution of food products to public institutions (except the military) and to schools, failed to carry this Johnson story, so that in this instance Johnson was hailed by the New York *Times* (April 5, 1944) while being ignored by, for instance, the Dallas *News* back home.

EGG BUYING PRICES SET FOR DRYING PLANTS

$9 Per Case, or 30c Per Dozen, Fixed Under U. S. Contracts

Special to THE NEW YORK TIMES.

WASHINGTON, April 4—Egg-drying establishments under contract to the War Food Administration are expected to pay not less than $9 a case, or 30 cents a dozen, for the eggs that they purchase for processing, Lee Marshall, Director of Food Distribution, warned today in telegrams sent to all plants holding Government contracts for powdered eggs. The minimum price specified is the national average support price for eggs announced by the WFA some time ago.

Mr. Marshall acted after reports reached WFA that many egg-drying plants were beating down prices for fresh eggs that they purchased from suppliers. Some of the reports, particularly those from mid-West egg-producing areas, indicated that egg-dryers were taking advantage of the heavy supply of fresh eggs and purchasing sup-

THE 15TH YEAR – 1945

On December 29, 1845, Texas became the twenty-eighth state in the Union. In the Texas Capitol one hundred years later a galaxy of Texas leaders gathered to commemorate the event, including the Congressman from the Tenth District. Johnson's speech was hardly three minutes long, but in that short span he reemphasized the Emersonian doctrine that people should look back only to honor and greatness, but principally should look forward for progress. "If we kneel at the shrine of the status quo," he said, then vision sees only a tunnel view.

Ironically, Congressman Johnson had one other function on this occasion—to introduce the man who would give him the most memorable race of his political life, the governor of Texas, who fought him to the wire, and then beyond, in the Senatorial affray of 1948, Coke R. Stevenson. Appropriately, Johnson said that Stevenson "needs no introduction to a Texas audience"!

Look again through those tall windows. Look far enough and you will see shining airplanes ... triumphantly marching men ... proud ships. Men who have tasted the wine of victory. Men who are marching home. And men who having tasted achievement will never again be content with the mild tea of generous promises.

In the hills and prairies of Texas ... are men ... women and children, some who have not been allowed the advantages of our science. They have not been given those blessings foreseen by our ancestors who visioned this great State. In a democracy the greatest cannot rise far above the most humble. Were those men alive today who formed Texas they would say to us ...

Lead our people up ... and up. Bring to them education ... sound minds in sound bodies. For the progress of men is limited only by the backwardness of other men.

THE 16TH YEAR – 1946

World War II had been terminated for seven months when Lyndon B. Johnson arose in the House of Representatives to deliver a speech entitled, "Not That Men Shall Die, But That Men May Live." As often happened in his career, his address foreshadowed one of his major problems of two decades later—the right of every American to proper health care. At the time probably most of the nation and certainly most of Congress shied away from what opponents called socialized medicine, a shibboleth that endured to drive many people away from understanding the minimal aspects of the proposed federal assistance to health care. While President Harry S. Truman favored such a program, firm supporters like Congressman Johnson were too sparsely spaced. But Johnson saw the issue of socialized medicine as essentially false. In the understandable terms he often used, "the fly which eats at the open privy of a slum area has no scruples about carrying polio to the child in the silk-stocking area . . . . The health of a community can be no better than the health of those least able to afford medical and hospital care."

S. 191 proposes to appropriate seventy-five millions a year for 5 years for the purpose of assisting the States to build proper hospital facilities. When you divide seventy-five millions among 48 States, and several Territories, the amount for each State is small indeed. As I said, it is a crawling step. But at least it is a step.

I shall not go into the intricacies of the matching plan at this time. I would call your attention to this fact. This is no attempt to federalize the Nation's hospitals. Once a hospital has been constructed with the aid set up in this bill, no Federal employee has the right to exercise supervision or control over its operations.

TEXAS SHORT 1,400 DOCTORS

Right here I should like to interject this thought. Before the Congress starts talking about socialized medicine, we ought to get enough doctors to take care of our people. It wouldn't do much good to have a card entitling you to medical service if there is no doctor to furnish that service.

The fact is that we have right now an acute shortage not only of hospital facilities but of doctors and nurses. In Texas, as an example because I know about Texas, we need 7,000 doctors for our population; we have fifty-six hundred. We are short fourteen hundred. The same picture prevails as to nurses. I think all of the talk about socializing medicine is nonsense and should be laid on the table until we train enough doctors and enough nurses and build enough hospitals. Unhappily, those are things you do not do overnight.

THE 17TH YEAR – 1947

One of the rules of politics is that the pendulum necessarily swings and that the outer reaches of the arc of the pendulum must regularly be corrected lest it swing too far. In post-World War II America majority feeling held that in business-labor relations the pendulum was now weighted in favor of organized labor. Accordingly, the Taft-Hartley bill, designed to place certain restraints on labor, passed both houses, only to be shot down by President Truman in a scorching veto message. Unlike love, re-passage of Taft-Hartley was no sweeter the second time around, as recriminations flowed from both sides. Congressman Johnson, who had withstood severe pressure when he voted with organized labor for the first minimum wage bill almost a decade ago, now resisted pressure from his labor friends and ran counter to his President's obvious wishes by voting his 1947 convictions. Johnson's stand nearly cost him the senatorial contest of 1948, as labor sought to defeat every Congressional supporter of the Taft-Hartley Act. This was one issue on which every congressman would lose friends, and Johnson proved no exception. Later labor forgave him and became a substantial supporter.

Bloc Delays Senate Vote on Labor Bill

Grim Group Wants Full Impact to Reach Nation

WASHINGTON, June 20 —(AP)—President Truman and Senator Taft (R-Ohio) slugged out a furious new round of debate over the labor bill Friday night while a little group of senators grimly held off a vote which could enact it over a veto.

The House already had voted overwhelmingly to override the President and put the bill on the lawbooks. But foes of the measure had the Senate tied up in a bickering, long night session when the Democratic President and the Republican chieftain laid their final arguments before the nation by radio.

Truman: The bill is "shocking," it would "undermine" collective bargaining, it would increase industrial strife, it would sow "seeds of discord" that would impair the country's unity and strength.

Taft: The President's veto message was "a complete misrepresentation," it "shows that he knows practically nothing about the bill," and he has "apparently adopted in large part the prejudiced arguments of the union leaders."

As the Senate headed into a night session, Senator Sparkman (D-Ala) announced that he will switch over and vote to uphold the veto. He had voted for the bill when the Senate passed it, but now he expressed agreement with the President's contention that it would "inject the

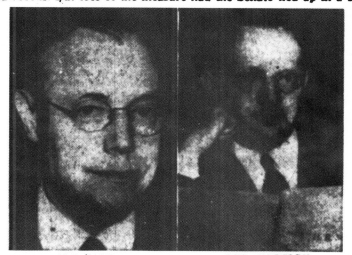

SEN. TAFT   REP. HARTLEY
Their bill called "Dangerous" and "Drastic"

Truman, Taft Swap Hot Words As Fight Is Radioed to People

WASHINGTON, June 20.—(UP)—President Truman carried to the people Friday night a stout defense of his veto of the Taft-Hartley Labor Control Bill. Senator Robert A. Taft (R-Ohio), countered immediately with a charge that he had "misrepresented" the issue.

The President, denouncing the bill as "shocking" and "deliberately designed to weaken labor unions, addressed a nationwide radio audience at 8 p. m. CST—nine hours after the House had overridden his veto by a margin of almost 4 to 1.

Taft, co-sponsor of the measure with Representative Fred A. Hart-

Veto Action Condemned And Hailed

HOW TEXANS VOTED ON OVERRIDING

WASHINGTON, June 20—(UP)—The roll call vote on overriding the President's veto of the labor bill includes:

For overriding: Beckworth, Wilson, Pickett, Teague, Johnson, Poague, Lucas, Gossett, Lyle, West, Burleson, Worley, Mahon, Fisher.

Against overriding: Rayburn, Thomas, Thomason.

government into private economic affairs on an unprecedented scale."

Suggests Vote Thursday

And senators fighting the bill to the last ditch made it clear that full impact of this veto gets across to the country," as Senator Taylor (D-Idaho) put it. He mentioned next Thursday for a vote.

Senator Morse (R-Ore.) similarly

THE 18TH YEAR – 1948

The year 1948 was an exciting one for Lyndon Johnson at both the national and the personal levels. Could the United States be spared a repetition of its disastrous retreat into that policy of passive concern that had followed World War I? Could America avoid the postwar depression-inflation cycle that had befallen that earlier world, especially as controls over rents and foodstuffs were removed? The Congressman from the Tenth District thought so, said so frequently, and voted accordingly. Particularly he supported President Truman in the latter's precedent-shattering assistance to Greece and Turkey—the so-called Truman Doctrine—and in his Marshall Plan for the recovery of Europe. From a political standpoint, 1948 was a dangerous year to lay beliefs on the voting line, for Truman's support in Congress, in his party, and with his nation was shaky; but beyond that, Lyndon Johnson was reaching again for the Senate rung in that now-famous campaign against Coke Stevenson, which placed Johnson in the Senate—and on his way to the Presidency—by such a narrow margin that forever after he took pride in calling himself "Landslide Lyndon."

THERE WILL BE HOPE FOR PEACE

Mr. JOHNSON of Texas. Mr. Speaker, the long hours of debate on this legislation are nearly ended, and soon this House will be called upon to vote "yes" or "no," on this program of financial aid to the free nations of the world across the seas.

No parliament of man ever before was confronted with a decision of more importance, for when we vote we will be voting "yes" or "no" upon the future of the human race.

If the vote is "yes," there will be hope for peace.

I would prefer to strike out that word "hope." I wish that I could say an affirmative vote on this measure would mean peace. In all honesty, that cannot be said. Our expenditure of this money is a gamble—the most heroic gamble in the history of mankind. Therefore, we can only hope that this will secure the peace.

THE SAFER RISK

But this is no reason for weak-hearted men to cower and retreat and run pell-mell away from destiny. In this world of violence, any course our Nation might take would be a gamble.

The course outlined in this legislation is, I believe, the safer risk.

If the vote should be "no," civilization would turn down the short and terrifying dead-end street of atomic warfare. From that path there would be no return.

● ● ●

This legislation was not written in Moscow.

This legislation was not written in Wall Street.

It was written on the Main Streets of America.

This legislation is what the great majority of the American public demands as minimum security for this hard-earned peace which we now hold so tentatively within our grasp.

● ● ●

Why is this vote so important? Why does so much hinge upon the appropriation of some $6,000,000,000 for aid to countries abroad?

The answer is this: For the first time in the history of the world a great Nation will, if this foreign aid bill becomes law, attempt to wage peace.

THE 19TH YEAR – 1949

Private Felix Longoria, born on April 19, 1919, began active military service on the anniversary of an old armistice, November 11, 1944, and died in the last months of action in the Philippines on June 16, 1945. To a New York *Times* correspondent, William S. White, Johnson explained: "I am sorry . . . . But there is, after all, a fine national funeral home, though of a rather different sort, out at Arlington." In defense of the *town* of Three Rivers, the city fathers raised money to send the soldier's father to the funeral, while in neighboring Corpus Christi the American GI Forum under Dr. Hector Garcia sent his widow. For this simple act of kindness Johnson received international publicity, most notably in Latin America. The New York *Times* devoted parts of three columns to its first account, both country and metropolitan newspapers editorialized favorably, and various ex-soldiers' organizations cited the new junior Senator from Texas. Philosophically and politically the freshman Senator was also serving a broad audience of average people, particularly in his uphill but successful and noticeable support of such Truman-sponsored public power bills as the Columbia Valley Administration and the Bonneville Power Administration.

Mexican GI To Be Buried At Arlington

A GI of Mexican ancestry who has been denied reburial facilities in his home town of Three Rivers, Tex., will be buried with military honors in Arlington National Cemetery.

Senator Lyndon B. Johnson (D., Tex.), said yesterday he arranged for the reburial after he was advised by the American GI Forum in Corpus Christi, Tex., that a Three Rivers funeral home had refused to handle the soldier's remains, "solely because of his Mexican ancestry."

The GI, Felix Lonforia, died in action on Luzon, in the Philippines.

The Senator said Dr. Hector Garcia, president of the Forum, told him in a telegram that the funeral home refused service because "other white people might object to use of the funeral home by people of Mexican origin."

Johnson arranged for Longoria's reinterment, without cost, either in Arlington or in Fort Sam Houston National Military Cemetery at San Antonia.

Mrs. Beatrice Longoria, the soldier's widow, notified the Senator she prefers Arlington.

The soldier's remains are scheduled to arrive via Army transport at San Francisco today. Final arrangements have not been completed.

Senator Johnson told Dr. Garcia: "I deeply regret to learn that the prejudice of some individuals extends even beyond this life.

THE 20TH YEAR – 1950

Since Lyndon Johnson had fought the battle of the personal budget from boyhood into the halls of Congress, he identified with those persons and institutions who have to struggle to stay abreast economically. Whether the concern was the rise in cost of outfitting a division from its World War II level of $15 million to the Korean plateau of $74 million just five years later; or whether it was a head of family's fight to provide rent and eggs in a period of rising prices, the Senator worked hard at trying to keep down prices. Once again, he was crossing the grain of President Truman, whose views prevailed, but typically Johnson had his eye on the consumer, a man for whom he would produce significant breakthroughs once Johnson became President.

Home Front Laxity Scored by Johnson

Washington Bureau of The News

WASHINGTON, Aug. 6. — In apparent impatience with the administration, Sen. Lyndon B. Johnson Sunday night decried "some (who) have been too timid, too hesitant, too slow in recognizing the need for home-front economic preparedness."

Johnson, in a speech broadcast over Texas stations, called economic preparedness "the forgotten front of the present struggle," and said

"Bravery on the fighting front is futile if cowardice and timidity have the upper hand on the home front."

Calling for a policy to make this country "the arsenal for the free world . . . now," Johnson said "anybody with open eyes can see what is coming."

In two world wars, he said "we bumbled and bungled our way through the battle of the home front."

Urging "profit from the errors of the past," he urged "as promptly as possible" that Congress pass standby controls for prices, wages and manpower, and high excess profits taxes.

"Equal sacrifice from all at the same time," Johnson said was necessary.

Johnson urged that an "automatic" controls program be approved, to avert its becoming "a political football."

Under the automatic feature, the controls on prices and wages would go into effect as soon as the cost of living index reached a certain point, regardless of any other administrative or congressional action.

Inflation, Johnson said, hits taxpayers twice — once in their own expenses and again when the government purchases at higher cost and has to get additional taxes to pay the bill.

A recent increase in prices on Navy airplanes, he said, cost the taxpayers $500,000.

Such instances, he said, would be multiplied as prices go up on other items "from the roast beef the troops eat to the coffee they drink, the tires on which they ride and the clothing they wear on their backs."

The Texan said it didn't make sense to raise more taxes to cover increasing prices. The sensible thing was to control prices and keep the amount of taxes in check.

Johnson reminded his Texas listeners that "Joe Stalin's Communists, not President Truman, were responsible for the invasion of South Korea. The quicker we direct our hostility to the enemy and not at our leaders, the quicker we will get the job done."

Johnson has consistently asked for more home-front preparedness and greater economic controls. He said originally that Mr. Truman's economic program did not go far enough.

THE 21ST YEAR – 1951

Involvement in Korea plus commitments in Europe and elsewhere caused considerable concern for the status of the United States' ability to defend itself as well as its striking power. In the Senate the Armed Forces Committee created a special Preparedness Subcommittee under Senator Johnson which investigated and analyzed every which way in its effort to gauge the nation's comparative military position. First studies were devoted to manpower and materials, and involved examination of contracts from General Motors to small college ROTC units. Johnson was especially concerned that no 18-year-old draftees be sent to Korea until every last possible older soldier and sailor had been utilized in the fighting units.

It may be that the Armed Services Committee and its Preparedness Subcommittee have not investigated everything the Senator from Minnesota would like to have us investigate. But all he needs to do, in order to have studied any subject within the purview of the Preparedness Subcommittee is to refer it to us. We have now many studies under way. It has been the feeling of the Senator from Texas that in the 12 months during which we have operated, with the 30 reports which we have submitted, going into the efficiency of operation of the Defense Department, going into its procurement and its contracts, going into its housing, and going into its utilization of manpower, we have served the purpose for which we were created.

THE 22ND YEAR – 1952

The elected public servant holds an ambiguous position. On the one hand he leads his constituency, while on the other, he represents their beliefs and interests. No doubt existed where most Texans stood on the issue of who should control the offshore lands of coastline states, with their potential of oil reserves and resultant tax returns. Texas did, in its overwhelming opinion, and as a result the senior Senator from Texas and his junior colleague, Price Daniel, led the national fight for states like California, Louisiana, and Florida to push through an act that would restore titles to the tidelands to the individual states. For Johnson it meant a head-on confrontation with his President and friend, Harry S. Truman, no slouch of a battler himself. As shown by this Dallas *News* article of May 20, 1952, Johnson could take off the gloves himself. In the bare-knuckle fight that ensued Johnson—and Texas—won; Truman—and the nation—lost. The fact that Texas tidelands alone have produced over $191,000,000 in revenue from 1953 to the end of August 1972 indicates the size of the stakes.

JOHNSON BLASTS TIDELANDS TALK

By WALTER C. HORNADAY

Washington Bureau of The News

WASHINGTON, May 19 — Sen Lyndon B. Johnson Monday attacked President Truman's Saturday night speech on tidelands legislation as "reckless," intemperate" and "unusual."

The President told the Americans for Democratic Action that the bill restoring the tidelands to the states represented "robbery in broad daylight, and on a colossal scale."

"There is robbery involved in this issue," Johnson told the Senate, "but who is robbing whom?

"The states that seek to protect their own property or the federal bureaucracy that seeks to take it away from them?"

Johnson declared he didn't think Senators "are going to be influenced by intemperate language or intimidated by political statements" in acting on overriding a veto.

President Truman informed congressional leaders Monday he will veto the bill, and promised to give at least two days notice, so advocates of state ownership and the opposition will have time to muster their full strength on an attempt to override.

The Senate will act first, because it was a Senate-designated bill that went to the White House. Speaker Sam Rayburn has predicted the House will easily override. The big question is the Senate.

Johnson's speech was part of a general attack in the Senate on the President's ADA address, in which he lashed out at some Republicans by name and took cracks at Gen. Dwight D. Eisenhower.

Sen. Pat McCarran (Dem) of Nevada, also joined in the criticism of President Truman, particularly for his statements about the tidelands bill.

Sen. Herman Welker (Rep) of Idaho, accused Mr Truman of telling an "utter and complete falsehood" when he linked Welker with an attack on Sen Alexander Wiley (Rep) of Wisconsin, for advocating a bipartisan foreign policy. Welker said he has asked the President to retract his statement.

Sen. B. B. Hickenlooper (Rep) of Iowa, also was critical of the President.

Johnson pointed out that it was unusual for the President to communicate directly to Congress on his legislative views, and giving them to a "private organization" first.

The Texas Senator said that Texas has considered the submerged coastal area part of its public domain for more than 100 years.

"That viewpoint has been upheld by international treaty, three justices of the Supreme Court of the United States, the National Association of Attorneys General, the Governors Conference, an overwhelming majority of the members of the House of Representatives and a substantial majority of the United States Senate," he asserted.

"The tidelands legislation would confirm what all these people held —that the submerged lands belong

See TIDELANDS, Page 12, Col 3

THE 23RD YEAR – 1953

As Senate Minority Leader, the youngest in history, Lyndon B. Johnson felt that the time had come for younger Senators to have choice committee assignments without waiting till they were hoary with age and service. Accordingly, he acted, to the delight of most and the dismay of a few who felt a first allegiance to seniority. Thus Democrats and Republicans alike, who otherwise would have waited years to get major assignments, benefited. And in the years ahead Senators as diverse as John F. Kennedy, Gale McGee, Edmund Muskie, J. William Fulbright, and Hubert Humphrey would retain a measure of gratitude to Johnson for having first set them on their respective roads to significant activity and ultimately to national prominence, with accompanying benefits for the nation as a whole. As Senator Alexander Wiley of Wisconsin, a ranking Republican, would note later, "I marveled at the way he would smile at Republicans and Democrats alike." Here in a press conference President Truman is commending the new Senate Minority Leader for having broken the slow advancement process of important senatorial committee service.

[12.] Q. Mr. President, the new Democratic leader, Senator Johnson of the Steering Committee,[8] has broken with some tradition and precedent on the Hill, to put freshmen Members on major committees, to see that each freshman got one important committee——

THE PRESIDENT. I think that is right and correct.

Q. Do you think that is a good thing?

THE PRESIDENT. I think it's a good thing. I was very lucky. When I went to the Senate I got three major committees. I was put on the Appropriations Committee, on the Interstate Commerce Committee——

Q. As a freshman?

THE PRESIDENT. ——on the Public Buildings and Grounds Committee. I was put on those three committees when I first got there, and not very long after that I was put on the Military Affairs Committee. So I think it's a good thing to have the membership of the committees fairly distributed. I don't think the Senators with seniority should hog all the good places on the good committees.

THE 24TH YEAR – 1954

Two emotional issues dominated this year. One concerned the decision handed down by the Supreme Court outlawing segregation in public schools. To that controversy Senator Johnson said simply that "the decision is an accomplished fact. . . . I have unlimited confidence in the ability of our people to work this matter out. . . in a manner that will be satisfactory to both races. This is the time for wisdom and for sound judgment." The other issue concerned the censure of Senator Joseph McCarthy. As Minority Leader, Senator Johnson operated under constant bombardment, particularly by fellow Democrats, to blast the noisome, often noxious Senator from Wisconsin. Johnson was denigrated by many members of his party because he would not participate in the name-calling. In this instance the Minority Leader played a well-known Johnson hand, extremely close to the vest, felt but not seen. Instead of confronting Senator McCarthy head-on, Johnson outflanked his aggressive colleague while he waited for McCarthy to hang himself. When the moment came, Johnson helped arrange the select committee which investigated McCarthy and heaped public praise on its chairman, Senator Arthur Watkins. The subsequent political demise of Senator McCarthy would seem to justify the Minority Leader's quiet but crafty approach.

The **PRESIDING OFFICER.** The Senator from Texas is recognized.

Mr. JOHNSON of Texas. At the outset of the debate it was my intention not to address the Senate on the subject now before the Senate.

I had thought that the question could best be handled through a calm discussion by the participants—the members of our select committee and the declared opponents of the resolution. The senior Senator from Texas believed it would be best to listen to the arguments advanced by the opposing sides, and then express his position by his vote alone.

After all, Mr. President, on an issue of this kind no person's word can be as eloquent as his vote.

Since the debate began, however, there have been developments which have changed my decision as to the course I should pursue. The most important is the attack made upon the select committee chosen by the majority and minority leaders, and I regard it as an attack upon the Senate itself.

THE 25TH YEAR – 1955

For all his famed penchant for knowing minute details in the most remote corners of his areas of concern, Lyndon Johnson always maintained a strong counterbalancing feeling about the sanctity of individual privacy. In his Presidential days he often endured criticism from forceful-minded people who wanted to utilize the many avenues available to the federal government to learn more about the private activities of the nation's citizenry. Here, as this transcript of an Eisenhower press conference indicates, Johnson is joining with other Congressional leaders and with President Eisenhower in restricting widespread Congressional delving into income tax returns.

Q. Edward P. Morgan, American Broadcasting Company: Mr. President, you have issued an order rather strictly restricting conditions under which congressional committees can get income tax returns. Can you tell us why this was done and whether it was to cover some specific situation?

THE PRESIDENT. No. It is a matter of the most delicate character. But the orders that I issued were completely coordinated with the chairmen of the committees that were affected by the order.[1] And so far as I know, they are completely satisfied with them.

Q. Donald J. Gonzales, United Press: Mr. President, has consideration been given to the placing of some additional ground forces, as such, on Formosa, even though we aren't going to put in a big base?

---

[1] The White House indicated after the news conference was completed that the coordination had been effected specifically with Senator Lyndon B. Johnson, Senate Majority Leader, Senator Harry F. Byrd, Chairman of the Senate Finance Committee, Representative Sam Rayburn, Speaker of the House, and Representative Jere Cooper, Chairman of the House Ways and Means Committee.

THE 26TH YEAR – 1956

By this year the Senate Majority Leader was an acclaimed national figure, credited with harmonizing the United States Senate so adeptly that its Democratic majority was moving in rhythm with its Republican President's progressive tempos and opposing only when Eisenhower seemed to be wandering offkey. It was an interesting year, with Eisenhower contesting for re-election; with Eisenhower and Johnson, among others, trying to liberalize immigration restrictions on victims of the Hungarian revolt against Russia; with the lingering shadow of Joe McCarthy still casting doubt across the land; with a pending civil rights bill seeming to push men of otherwise goodwill into extreme corners; and with Lyndon Johnson back at his post, driving himself and others, as hard as ever after being almost counted out of this world with his 1955 coronary. In San Antonio on July 7, as reported in the next day's Houston *Post*, Johnson performed another of those ritual services he enjoyed—and did so well. As he dedicated a new radio-TV station, he spoke out for non-conformity and for free presentation of facts. In view of the controversy encompassing the media nearly two decades later, his words have enormous contemporary pertinence.

Free Flow of Ideas Is Vital, Johnson Insists

SAN ANTONIO—(AP)—A call for unlimited exchange of ideas was sounded here Saturday afternoon by Sen Lyndon Johnson.

Johnson, speaking at the dedication of KENS TV and KENS Radio's new modern studios, saw the free exchange of ideas and the reasonable consideration of all ideas as vital for the survival of free institutions and the progress of the nation.

HUNDREDS OF guests inspected the new studio Saturday and heard the dedication addresses. Other Texas leaders and dignitaries joined in the dedication.

Johnson depicted the new studios as one of the symbols of the essential unity that a city must have if it is to survive.

"We are living in an age when the unity of Americans has become tremendously important," the senior Texas senator said. "It is more than a matter of making life pleasant. It is a matter of the survival of our free institutions and the progress of our people," he said.

"UNITY, HOWEVER, cannot be a mere matter of conformity. It must be based upon the free exchange of ideas and the reasonable consideration of all ideas. It must be founded upon the conclusions of men who have examined the facts and refused to rely solely upon their prejudices," Johnson said in his radio and television address.

"Our country is torn today between the tugging and the hauling of the right and the left. The extremists—on both sides—are few in number and represent no more than a minority of our people. But they have strengths which make up for their weaknesses," the senator said.

Most people reject the right and the left whenever they have the opportunity, Johnson said.

"THAT IS WHY this building is so very important," he said. "This is a source of facts —facts which will go to all the people in this area. And in the modern world, facts have become as important and as vital as food itself," Johnson said.

THE 27TH YEAR – 1957

When the last major civil rights law had been passed, Abraham Lincoln was a fresh martyr and Ulysses S. Grant the nation's newest hero (except for that one-third who clung to Robert E. Lee); slavery had just been closed down by a fratricidal war that would make America's role in future world wars and Koreas and Vietnams look like a comparative highway death toll over a long weekend; and transcontinental railroads, western cowboys, Sitting Bull, General Custer, and Wounded Knee were hunching somewhere in a shadowy future. But three quarters of a century of inaction ended with the successful steering by Johnson and Sam Rayburn through Congress of an idea whose time was overdue. As Hubert H. Humphrey, then one of the Senate firebrands, wrote to Johnson, "I was never more proud of you!" In turn, Johnson, who had insisted that if a civil rights bill weren't passed in 1957, years might pass before reason and sanity could be recaptured sufficiently to consider another such bill, observed, "I am today as proud of this great body . . . , as I have ever been. It has operated in its finest deliberative traditions." No one, whatever his views on civil rights, can deny that it was an historic session, nor that Lyndon Johnson had been the chief architect and engineer.

H. R. 6127

Eighty-fifth Congress of the United States of America

AT THE FIRST SESSION

Begun and held at the City of Washington on Thursday, the third day of January, one thousand nine hundred and fifty-seven

An Act

To provide means of further securing and protecting the civil rights of persons within the jurisdiction of the United States.

Be it enacted by the Senate and House of Representatives of the United States of America in Congress assembled,

PART I—ESTABLISHMENT OF THE COMMISSION ON CIVIL RIGHTS

SEC. 101. (a) There is created in the executive branch of the Government a Commission on Civil Rights (hereinafter called the "Commission").

(b) The Commission shall be composed of six members who shall be appointed by the President by and with the advice and consent of the Senate. Not more than three of the members shall at any one time be of the same political party.

(c) The President shall designate one of the members of the Commission as Chairman and one as Vice Chairman. The Vice Chairman shall act as Chairman in the absence or disability of the Chairman, or in the event of a vacancy in that office.

(d) Any vacancy in the Commission shall not affect its powers and shall be filled in the same manner, and subject to the same limitation with respect to party affiliations as the original appointment was made.

(e) Four members of the Commission shall constitute a quorum.

RULES OF PROCEDURE OF THE COMMISSION

SEC. 102. (a) The Chairman or one designated by him to act as Chairman at a hearing of the Commission shall announce in an opening statement the subject of the hearing.

(b) A copy of the Commission's rules shall be made available to the witness before the Commission.

(c) Witnesses at the hearings may be accompanied by their own counsel for the purpose of advising them concerning their constitutional rights.

(d) The Chairman or Acting Chairman may punish breaches of order and decorum and unprofessional ethics on the part of counsel, by censure and exclusion from the hearings.

(e) If the Commission determines that evidence or testimony at any hearing may tend to defame, degrade, or incriminate any person, it shall (1) receive such evidence or testimony in executive session;

THE 28TH YEAR – 1958

When the Russians announced that they had successfully thrust a satellite into orbit around the earth, many Americans, private and public, succumbed to near-hysteria. Indisputably, the United States had been caught in second-place, and to that part of the American nation interested in space and missiles, second-place represented no place at all. But in Washington some leaders bowed their necks, determined to take whatever steps would restore American leadership. Among these was the Senate Majority Leader, who within a few months had formed another select committee, this time on space, with himself as chairman. Shortly he had drafted and passed the necessary legislation to create NASA, as well as the National Aeronautics and Space Council, both under civilian control. No scientist, Johnson is nonetheless recognized as one of the fathers of the United States space program. As Senator Philip Hart later said, "Certainly [historians] will identify Lyndon B. Johnson as one who first saw and persuaded Congress to see that this earth has become just a tiny star in the vastness of conquerable space; who now guides our steps into space—giant and peaceful steps." Toward the end of that first fretful year, when the New York Institute of Technology presented Johnson with its first national service award, he included in his acceptance speech the accompanying remarks about the potentials of space for creating peace.

**ADDRESS BY SENATE DEMOCRATIC LEADER LYNDON B. JOHNSON
BEFORE NATIONAL TECHNOLOGY AWARDS AND FOUNDERS DINNER
OF NEW YORK INSTITUTE OF TECHNOLOGY, NEW YORK CITY
TUESDAY, DECEMBER 16, 1958, 7:00 p.m.**

● ● ● ●

Since time began, men have despised and deplored the
waste of war as free men do today. Yet the truth is that through the
centuries we have been more prodigal with peace than with war. We
have never yet used the resources of peace with any of the imagination
and resoluteness that we have applied to the resources of war. That
is the challenge before the world at this hour.

This is so for one reason.

That reason is space.

The realms of space open to us--for the first time--
a rich and untapped deposit of these resources of peace. Here
within man's reach, at last, is a true capability for peace.

I speak less figuratively than it may seem.

Our talk of space today is largely the field talk of a
surveying crew. We are concerned with landmarks and distances
and characteristics of a new terrain. There has not yet begun to
appear in our awareness much sense of what lies immediately
beyond this present making of maps.

We know already, though, that within a decade, by the
late 1960's, there can be and will be systems of communications
satellites and weather satellites and navigational satellites orbiting
about us.

Worldwide television will be an everyday affair.

International telephone and radio communications will be
as common and about as economical as "long distance" today.

Global weather forecasting--far more accurate and far
more advanced than now--will be standard.

Ships of the seas will steer by satellite signals.

More important than these techniques will be the changes
wrought here on earth. The technology which produces these achievements out in space will produce here among nations and men the most
dramatic change yet experienced.

Whole new sciences will come into being within ten years.

Whole new industries will be created.

THE 29TH YEAR – 1959

After decades of trying, Alaska and Hawaii were admitted to the Union as the 49th and 50th states, the first to be added since Arizona in 1912. The roads had been long, tortuous, and tortured. Hawaii had first formally petitioned more than a half-century before, in 1903; while Delegate James Wickersham had first introduced an Alaskan statehood bill on the eve of America's entry into the First World War, 1916. But always statehood for the two territories had been frustrated until Lyndon Johnson and Sam Rayburn had demonstrated their political healing skills to guide through to completion the two statehood acts, both promptly proclaimed by President Eisenhower in 1959. As Senator E. L. (Bob) Bartlett, one of Alaska's first two Senators, said to Vice President Johnson in 1962, "if it had not been for you and for Speaker Rayburn, Alaska would not now be a State;" while Senator Oren E. Long of Hawaii stated, "when statehood for Hawaii became an accomplished fact it was due . . . overwhelmingly—to the driving interest and purpose of [Senator Johnson]. We shall never forget it."

3 ¶ Remarks Upon Signing the Proclamation Admitting Alaska to the Union and the Executive Order Changing the Flag of the United States. *January* 3, 1959

GENTLEMEN, I think that all of us recognize this as an historic occasion. Certainly for myself I feel very highly privileged and honored to welcome the forty-ninth State into the Union.

Such a ceremony has not taken place in almost half a century, so at least I have the feeling of self-gratification that I am not just one of a group in this kind of ceremony.

To the State itself, to its people, I extend on behalf of all their sister States, best wishes and hope for prosperity and success. And to each of you gentlemen elected to high office to represent your new State, in both State and Federal offices, my congratulations, my felicitations, and my hope that we will all work together to the benefit of all forty-nine States.

• • • •

60 ¶ Statement by the President Upon Signing the Hawaii Statehood Bill. *March* 18, 1959

IT HAS given me great satisfaction to sign the Act providing for the admission of Hawaii into the Union.

Since my inauguration in 1953 I have consistently urged that this legislation be enacted, so the action of the Congress so early in this session is most gratifying.

Under this legislation, the citizens of Hawaii will soon decide whether their Islands shall become our fiftieth State. In so doing, they will demonstrate anew to the world the vitality of the principles of freedom and self-determination—the principles upon which this Nation was founded 172 years ago.

THE 30TH YEAR – 1960

Though he was slow in announcing, Lyndon Johnson was considered a strong candidate for the Democratic nomination for President in 1960. However, astute political observers felt that the John F. Kennedy partisans had done a superior pre-convention job of canvassing delegate votes and that Johnson's only chance would come if the convention went beyond the first ballot. In general, no one thought that Johnson would accept the No. 2 spot on the Democratic ticket, because the Senator's position as Majority Leader had become the second most powerful office in the federal government. When Kennedy won on the first ballot and then offered the Vice Presidential nomination to Johnson, politically shrewd friends like Speaker Sam Rayburn (who later changed his mind) advised against his "stepping down." But Johnson, always a loyal party man, felt with Kennedy that his presence on the ticket was essential to hold in line a recalcitrant South. In the Kennedy victory that followed, even the most fervid Johnson detractors in the Kennedy entourage agreed that Johnson's vote-getting abilities had been crucial in returning the Presidency to the Democrats. For the success of his party and its program, in which he believed, he had surrendered power and subordinated himself. When he told the Los Angeles *Times* reporter on that night of his nomination that he was "proud" to be Kennedy's running mate, he was not indulging in political cliche! He was indeed proud because he thought that his place on the ticket would help translate desirable party policies into national policies.

Johnson 'Proud' to Be Kennedy's Running Mate, Predicts Victory

BY GENE BLAKE

Sen. Johnson of Texas said yesterday he is proud to accept Sen. Kennedy's recommendation of him as a Vice Presidential running mate.

"I neither sought nor solicited that (Kennedy's)

Illustrated on Page B

statement and recommendation or anyone's support for the Vice Presidency," Johnson said.

"As I have said many times, I do not think any man has the right to refuse to serve his country if he is convinced he can serve."

Johnson was in the midst of entertaining many prominent governors, senators and congressmen in his Biltmore suite when Kennedy made his announcement.

He and his wife, Lady Bird, stepped out into the hall jammed with newsmen and climbed onto chairs to make a statement.

"I stated to Sen. Kennedy that I thought he was entitled as the overwhelming favorite of this convention to decide on the individuals he would like to run with him or serve with him as our commander in chief," Johnson said.

"I suggested that once he made that determination he should make known his decision to the people of the country and to the delegates at the convention.

"Sen. Kennedy told me he desired to recommend that I accept the nomination if it is offered on his recommendation.

"I will support the platform and stump this country with Sen. Kennedy from coast to coast in an attempt to win a Democratic victory in November."

After joining Sen. Kennedy later for pictures, Johnson was pressed for further clarification on why he had agreed to accept second place on the ticket.

"The Presidential nominee asked me to accept second place on the ticket," he replied.

Denies Pressure

"He and a great many other leaders thought my experience and leadership of the Senate would be valuable in the constitutional duties of the Vice President. After giving the matter careful consideration, I thought it was my duty to accept."

Johnson was asked about reports that considerable pressure was exerted on him.

"That is not true," he said. "I am very proud to be on the ticket. I am not very easy to pressure."

Observers noted, however, that after Kennedy first

Please Turn to Pg. 6. Col. 1

THE 31ST YEAR – 1961

Since John F. Kennedy knew that he had a Vice President who chafed under inactivity, he sought ways to enlist Johnson's huge energies and vast experience. One avenue was by representing Kennedy abroad on missions ranging from the ceremonial to the diplomatically delicate. No trip proved more successful than the symbolic mission to Berlin, made shortly after the Communists had built the infamous wall separating East and West Berlin. In the shadow of that wall, before cheering multitudes, Johnson reasserted the dedication of the United States to the continued freedom of West Berliners and West Germans. Two days after the New York *Times* (August 20) published this lead story on Johnson's impact, it carried another lead story in which President Kennedy, with the first diplomatic reports in hand, hailed Johnson for his service to world peace and his triumphal advancement of the principle of liberty of choice.

JOHNSON HAILED IN WEST BERLIN AS HE RENEWS PLEDGE OF U.S. AID; SOVIET REJECTS ALLIES' PROTEST

300,000 APPLAUD

Vice President Tells Them Washington Will Not Forget

Address to the West Berlin Parliament is on Page 4.

By SYDNEY GRUSON
Special to The New York Times

BERLIN, Aug. 19 — Vice President Johnson pledged to the people of West Berlin today that the United States would never forget its obligations to them.

This was the heart of three speeches the Vice President made shortly after arriving here on a mission for President Kennedy to reassure West Germany and West Berlin.

In an address at a special meeting of the West Berlin Parliament, the Vice President said:

"To the survival and to the creative future of this city we Americans have pledged, in effect, what our ancestors pledged in forming the United States.

'Our lives, our fortunes and our sacred honor.' "

These are the final words of the Declaration of Independence.

Mr. Johnson's presence and his words had an electric effect on the city. There were tears and cheers as he spoke to a crowd estimated at 300,000 persons massed in the square in front of the City Hall.

Cheers on 8-Mile Route

There was a near mob scene as he got out of his car on the ride to the City Hall from the airport to shake hands with a few of the 100,000 others who braved intermittent rain to cheer him along the eight-mile route.

The city was like a boxer who had thrown off a heavy punch and was gathering stamina for another round.

The punch was the Communists' closing of the border at midnight between East and West Berlin last Saturday and the long delay in Western reaction, a delay that was made doubly bitter when the first reaction was confined to a protest note.

The Vice President said nothing essentially new. That did not seem to matter. The West Berliners wanted the words said at

THE 32ND YEAR – 1962

Probably the most important domestic contributions of Vice President Johnson evolved from his chairmanships of the National Aeronautical and Space Council, the President's Committee on Equal Employment Opportunity, and the Peace Corps Advisory Committee, as well as membership on the National Security Council. To Johnson, these appointments did not represent window-dressing but working assignments. As the New York *Times* of June 18 indicates here, Johnson meant business when he talked about spreading equal employment opportunities. Two days after this story appeared, Johnson replied with a column-long, twelve-paragraph letter to the editor in which he said that "Controversy, like beauty, is frequently in the eye of the beholder . . . as far as I am concerned the objective of the committee is to insure equal employment opportunity for all of our citizens . . . based upon considerations of both wisdom and morality." After explaining the legal limitations upon his program, he asserted that his committee had gone "beyond the policing functions of the executive order . . . to build other positive programs which will speed progress toward our goal." His committee sought compliance with equal employment opportunity tenets in federal contracts, urged voluntary programs by employers, negotiated with trade unions to promote non-discrimination, and tried to persuade people in local communities to provide training "that qualifies a man to compete for a job on a basis of equality with his fellow man." He closed with this declaration: "It is my intention to sponsor any and every legitimate form of action that will produce results." That he did.

Johnson's Committee on Jobs for Negroes

N. A. A. C. P. FEARS DRIVE MAY FALTER

But Vice President's Aides and Labor Secretary Are Untroubled by Dispute

Continued From Page 1, Col. 4

disagreement in a group as varied as this one."

However, some civil rights groups, notably the National Association for the Advancement of Colored People, have expressed concern. They fear that Mr. Troutman's operation, if uncontrolled, will weaken the "hard line" originally laid down by the President.

Similar worries have been voiced privately by some committee members, notably John C. Wheeler, president of a Negro bank in Durham, N. C., and Walter P. Reuther, president of the United Automobile Workers.

The hard line was set out in the President's Executive Order of March, 1961, which created the Johnson panel and its thirty-five-man staff, headed by Mr. Feild, former executive director of Michigan's Fair Employment Practices Commission.

The panel was given the job of ending racial discrimination by Federal agencies and private concerns with Government contracts. Such discrimination was prohibited by the order.

Unlike its counterpart under Vice President Richard M. Nixon, the Johnson committee's

Theodore W. Kheel, who is studying the committee.

mandate had "teeth." The sharpest were a compliance reporting system for industry, active investigation of Negro complaints, and sanctions against recalcitrant employers, including contract cancellation.

65 Per Cent Settled

"We mean business," the Vice President has repeatedly told both industry and civil rights groups.

To date, under Mr. Johnson's supervision, Mr. Feild's office has received 870 complaints of discrimination by Government contractors and has settled 65 per cent of them, with the aid of other Federal agencies.

With considerable help from industry, the Feild staff has also slowly created an "equality control" system covering 300,000

THE 33RD YEAR – 1963

On November 22, 1963, the world was shocked when an assassin's bullet felled President John F. Kennedy. No one knew whether the murderer was acting alone or whether the President's death was part of a larger plot to destroy the leadership, perhaps the government, of the United States. In a time tailor-made for tumult and hysteria, the new President, Lyndon B. Johnson, represented an island of calm in a rolling sea; and the exchange of power—awesome power—from Kennedy to Johnson was accomplished with a minimum of disruption and confusion. For the next several weeks Johnson moved to reassure the nation, to reaffirm the principles in which Kennedy—and he—believed, and to reset the pulse of government to a forward functioning level. In that effort he met with Congress in joint session just five days after the assassination and "in this moment of new resolve" urged his fellow Americans: "let us continue."

We will carry on the fight against poverty and misery, and disease and ignorance, in other lands and in our own.

We will serve all the Nation, not one section or one sector, or one group, but all Americans. These are the United States—a united people with a united purpose.

Our American unity does not depend upon unanimity. We have differences; but now, as in the past, we can derive from those differences strength, not weakness, wisdom, not despair. Both as a people and a government, we can unite upon a program, a program which is wise and just, enlightened and constructive.

For 32 years Capitol Hill has been my home. I have shared many moments of pride with you, pride in the ability of the Congress of the United States to act, to meet any crisis, to distill from our differences strong programs of national action.

An assassin's bullet has thrust upon me the awesome burden of the Presidency. I am here today to say I need your help; I cannot bear this burden alone. I need the help of all Americans, and all America. This Nation has experienced a profound shock, and in this critical moment, it is our duty, yours and mine, as the Government of the United States, to do away with uncertainty and doubt and delay, and to show that we are capable of decisive action; that from the brutal loss of our leader we will derive not weakness, but strength; that we can and will act and act now.

From this chamber of representative government, let all the world know and none misunderstand that I rededicate this Government to the unswerving support of the United Nations, to the honorable and determined execution of our commitments to our allies, to the maintenance of military strength second to none, to the defense of the strength and the stability of the dollar, to the expansion of our foreign trade, to the reinforcement of our programs of mutual assistance and cooperation in Asia and Africa, and to our Alliance for Progress in this hemisphere.

On the 20th day of January, in 1961, John F. Kennedy told his countrymen that our national work would not be finished "in the first thousand days, nor in the life of this administration, nor even perhaps in our lifetime on this planet. But," he said, "let us begin."

Today, in this moment of new resolve, I would say to all my fellow Americans, let us continue.

This is our challenge—not to hesitate, not to pause, not to turn about and linger over this evil moment, but to continue on our course so that we may fulfill the destiny that history has set for us. Our most immediate tasks are here on this Hill.

First, no memorial oration or eulogy could more eloquently honor President Kennedy's memory than the earliest possible passage of the civil rights bill for which he fought so long. We have talked long enough in this country about equal rights. We have talked for one hundred years or more. It is time now to write the next chapter, and to write it in the books of law.

I urge you again, as I did in 1957 and again in 1960, to enact a civil rights law so that we can move forward to eliminate from this Nation every trace of discrimination and oppression that is based upon race or color. There could be no greater source of strength to this Nation both at home and abroad.

And second, no act of ours could more fittingly continue the work of President Kennedy than the early passage of the tax bill for which he fought all this long year. This is a bill designed to increase our national income and Federal revenues, and to provide insurance against recession. That bill, if passed without delay, means more security

THE 34TH YEAR – 1964

Any year with Lyndon Johnson at the center was a hyperactive year. The new President's first full year only displayed to the nation what his former colleagues, employees, and friends already knew—that when Johnson moved in, action followed. Bills long stalled in one or the other house of Congress were pried loose, and new bills followed hard on their heels. By the hundreds they were pushed through and signed by the President. They dealt with all phases of the Great Society—a National Wilderness Preservation System, disaster relief in Alaska, a National Council on the Arts (introduced just the previous January), income maintenance for cotton farmers, Canyonlands National Park, mass transportation systems, insured rental housing loans for the rural elderly, disposition of judgment funds to Chippewa and other Indian tribes, the Economic Opportunity Act (war on poverty), constitutional rights for the mentally ill, and extension of social security coverage. In this torrent of new legislation nothing pleased Johnson more—nor had wider implications—than HR 7152, which enforced the constitutional right to vote, outlawed discrimination in public accommodations and guaranteed equal rights in education, which the President signed just two days before the 188th anniversary of the Declaration of Independence, with its ringing proclamation that "all men are created free and equal."

Eighty-eighth Congress of the United States of America

AT THE SECOND SESSION

*Begun and held at the City of Washington on Tuesday, the seventh day of January,
one thousand nine hundred and sixty-four*

An Act

To enforce the constitutional right to vote, to confer jurisdiction upon the district courts of the United States to provide injunctive relief against discrimination in public accommodations, to authorize the Attorney General to institute suits to protect constitutional rights in public facilities and public education, to extend the Commission on Civil Rights, to prevent discrimination in federally assisted programs, to establish a Commission on Equal Employment Opportunity, and for other purposes.

Be it enacted by the Senate and House of Representatives of the United States of America in Congress assembled, That this Act may be cited as the "Civil Rights Act of 1964".

TITLE I—VOTING RIGHTS

SEC. 101. Section 2004 of the Revised Statutes (42 U.S.C. 1971), as amended by section 131 of the Civil Rights Act of 1957 (71 Stat. 637), and as further amended by section 601 of the Civil Rights Act of 1960 (74 Stat. 90), is further amended as follows:

(a) Insert "1" after "(a)" in subsection (a) and add at the end of subsection (a) the following new paragraphs:

"(2) No person acting under color of law shall—

"(A) in determining whether any individual is qualified under State law or laws to vote in any Federal election, apply any standard, practice, or procedure different from the standards, practices, or procedures applied under such law or laws to other individuals within the same county, parish, or similar political subdivision who have been found by State officials to be qualified to vote;

"(B) deny the right of any individual to vote in any Federal election because of an error or omission on any record or paper relating to any application, registration, or other act requisite to voting, if such error or omission is not material in determining whether such individual is qualified under State law to vote in such election; or

"(C) employ any literacy test as a qualification for voting in any Federal election unless (i) such test is administered to each individual and is conducted wholly in writing, and (ii) a certified copy of the test and of the answers given by the individual is furnished to him within twenty-five days of the submission of his request made within the period of time during which records and papers are required to be retained and preserved pursuant to title III of the Civil Rights Act of 1960 (42 U.S.C. 1974–74e; 74 Stat. 88) : *Provided, however,* That the Attorney General may enter into agreements with appropriate State or local authorities that preparation, conduct, and maintenance of such tests in accordance with the provisions of applicable State or local law, including such special provisions as are necessary in the preparation, conduct, and maintenance of such tests for persons who are blind or otherwise physically handicapped, meet the purposes of this subparagraph and constitute compliance therewith.

"(3) For purposes of this subsection—

"(A) the term 'vote' shall have the same meaning as in subsection (e) of this section;

"(B) the phrase 'literacy test' includes any test of the ability

THE 35TH YEAR – 1965

More hundreds of laws. Another landmark passed in civil rights with the Voting Rights Act, which the President signed in August. At last the XVth Amendment, ratified a century before, would be truly effective and firmly enforced. Other major acts, along with the lesser ones, each aimed at improving the quality of life in the United States: the Appalachian Regional Development Act, a tax cut, an Older Americans Act, a new Department of Housing and Urban Development, Assateague Island National Seashore, the National Foundation on the Arts and Humanities, the Federal Water Pollution Control Act, the re-opening of doors to immigration, standards for air pollution, highway beautification, the Higher Education Act, and the long-awaited consummation of medicare for the elderly, signed symbolically and sentimentally in the presence of former President Harry S. Truman in Independence, Missouri. What policy, what act mattered most, affected the most people, triggered the greater revolution or advance? ¿Quien sabe? But certainly the Elementary and Secondary Education Act, designed to strengthen and improve educational quality and educational opportunities, hit every parent and every child in the nation, not to mention generations in the future. Its passage marked the culmination of a dream born to a young teacher in Cotulla, Texas, more than a third of a century ago, who from his own meager salary bought books and playground equipment for Mexican students because the school system was too poor to provide. Lyndon Johnson saw no need for this kind of educational poverty to be perpetuated, and as President he used the power of the federal government to move as close as possible to equal educational opportunity.

Eighty-ninth Congress of the United States of America

AT THE FIRST SESSION

*Begun and held at the City of Washington on Monday, the fourth day of January,
one thousand nine hundred and sixty-five*

An Act

To strengthen and improve educational quality and educational opportunities
in the Nation's elementary and secondary schools.

*Be it enacted by the Senate and House of Representatives of the
United States of America in Congress assembled,* That this Act may
be cited as the "Elementary and Secondary Education Act of 1965".

TITLE I—FINANCIAL ASSISTANCE TO LOCAL EDUCA-
TIONAL AGENCIES FOR THE EDUCATION OF CHIL-
DREN OF LOW-INCOME FAMILIES AND EXTENSION
OF PUBLIC LAW 874, EIGHTY-FIRST CONGRESS

SEC. 2. The Act of September 30, 1950, Public Law 874, Eighty-first
Congress, as amended (20 U.S.C. 236–244), is amended by inserting:

"TITLE I—FINANCIAL ASSISTANCE FOR LOCAL EDUCA-
TIONAL AGENCIES IN AREAS AFFECTED BY FEDERAL
ACTIVITY"

immediately above the heading of section 1, by striking out "this Act"
wherever it appears in sections 1 through 6, inclusive (other than
where it appears in clause (B) of section 4(a)), and inserting in lieu
thereof "this title", and by adding immediately after section 6 the
following new title:

"TITLE II—FINANCIAL ASSISTANCE TO LOCAL EDUCA-
TIONAL AGENCIES FOR THE EDUCATION OF CHIL-
DREN OF LOW-INCOME FAMILIES

"DECLARATION OF POLICY

"SEC. 201. In recognition of the special educational needs of children of low-income families and the impact that concentrations of low-
income families have on the ability of local educational agencies to
support adequate educational programs, the Congress hereby declares
it to be the policy of the United States to provide financial assistance
(as set forth in this title) to local educational agencies serving areas
with concentrations of children from low-income families to expand
and improve their educational programs by various means (including
preschool programs) which contribute particularly to meeting the
special educational needs of educationally deprived children.

"KINDS AND DURATION OF GRANTS

"SEC. 202. The Commissioner shall, in accordance with the provisions of this title, make payments to State educational agencies for
basic grants to local educational agencies for the period beginning
July 1, 1965, and ending June 30, 1968, and he shall make payments to
State educational agencies for special incentive grants to local educational agencies for the period beginning July 1, 1966, and ending
June 30, 1968.

THE 36TH YEAR – 1966

Although foreign involvements, particularly in Vietnam, absorbed more and more of President Johnson's attention, he never flagged in his program for providing more service for his constituency, which by now had become international. Thus 1966 saw the passage of laws in such fields as food for India, child nutrition, model cities, rent supplements, clean rivers, food for freedom, safety (traffic, highway, tires, and mines, for instance), narcotics rehabilitation, international education, bail reform, minimum wage increase, urban mass transit, fish/wildlife preservation, scientific and cultural exchanges, and freedom of information, as well as the creation of such agencies as the Department of Transportation, Guadalupe National Park, and the Revolutionary War Bicentennial Commission, which was given a decade of lead time to prepare for the nation's 200th birthday. Probably the two laws that more nearly involved every American were the Fair Packaging and Labeling Act, popularly known as the Truth-in-Packaging Act, and the Child Protection Act. Both were aimed at safeguarding that most numerous of all people, the consumer. As Johnson said at their signing, the two acts were designed to "help the American housewife . . . save her pennies and dimes, and the American mother . . . save her children." Too long, the President felt, the consumer had needed "a yardstick or slide rule or computer" to ascertain whether labels lied, whether indeed the purchaser was buying what she was paying for. Now at last this "strong but simple law" required "the manufacturer to tell the shopper clearly and understandably exactly what is in the package, who made it, how much it contains, and how much it costs." As for the Child Protection Act, it banned "the sale of toys and other children's articles" that were "dangerous or deadly," as well as "other household articles so hazardous that even labels cannot make them safe:

"—Now there is a law that says the eyes of a doll will not be poisonous beans.

"—Now there is a law that says what looks like candy will not be deadly firecracker balls.

"—Now there is a law that says Johnny will not die because his toy truck was painted with a poison."

These then were not dramatic acts, but laws tinctured with compassion, laws whose "purpose is to uphold truth." And as the President told the people gathered at the signing, "We will look back . . . in the years to come and wonder, 'How did the Congress do this much before October?'"

Eighty-ninth Congress of the United States of America

AT THE SECOND SESSION

Begun and held at the City of Washington on Monday, the tenth day of January, one thousand nine hundred and sixty-six

An Act

To regulate interstate and foreign commerce by preventing the use of unfair or deceptive methods of packaging or labeling of certain consumer commodities distributed in such commerce, and for other purposes.

Be it enacted by the Senate and House of Representatives of the United States of America in Congress assembled, That this Act may be cited as the "Fair Packaging and Labeling Act".

DECLARATION OF POLICY

SEC. 2. Informed consumers are essential to the fair and efficient functioning of a free market economy. Packages and their labels should enable consumers to obtain accurate information as to the quantity of the contents and should facilitate value comparisons. Therefore, it is hereby declared to be the policy of the Congress to assist consumers and manufacturers in reaching these goals in the marketing of consumer goods.

PROHIBITION OF UNFAIR AND DECEPTIVE PACKAGING AND LABELING

SEC. 3. (a) It shall be unlawful for any person engaged in the packaging or labeling of any consumer commodity (as defined in this Act) for distribution in commerce, or for any person (other than a common carrier for hire, a contract carrier for hire, or a freight forwarder for hire) engaged in the distribution in commerce of any packaged or labeled consumer commodity, to distribute or to cause to be distributed in commerce any such commodity if such commodity is contained in a package, or if there is affixed to that commodity a label, which does not conform to the provisions of this Act and of regulations promulgated under the authority of this Act.

(b) The prohibition contained in subsection (a) shall not apply to persons engaged in business as wholesale or retail distributors of consumer commodities except to the extent that such persons (1) are engaged in the packaging or labeling of such commodities, or (2) prescribe or specify by any means the manner in which such commodities are packaged or labeled.

REQUIREMENTS AND PROHIBITIONS

SEC. 4. (a) No person subject to the prohibition contained in section 3 shall distribute or cause to be distributed in commerce any packaged consumer commodity unless in conformity with regulations which shall be established by the promulgating authority pursuant to section 6 of this Act which shall provide that—

(1) The commodity shall bear a label specifying the identity of the commodity and the name and place of business of the manufacturer, packer, or distributor;

(2) The net quantity of contents (in terms of weight, measure, or numerical count) shall be separately and accurately stated in a uniform location upon the principal display panel of that label;

(3) The separate label statement of net quantity of contents appearing upon or affixed to any package—

(A)(i) if on a package containing less than four pounds or one

THE 37TH YEAR – 1967

In the surge of laws and policies aimed at practical reforms, from the specifics of consumerism to the broad program of alleviating hunger in the world, Lyndon B. Johnson did not lose sight of the spirit. He put men to work on such intangibles as racism and violence, ignorance and personality disorders, and the effects of clean air and clean rivers and broad vistas on people harried by a crowding world. Two years before, at the signing of the Arts and Humanities bill, he had remarked that "The arts and the humanities belong to the people," and he talked regularly of "another essential human freedom . . . freedom from ignorance." Consequently, from his standpoint he was moving logically when he began to press for passage of a bill establishing a Corporation for Public Broadcasting, which became an actuality on November 7. He saw a generously endowed public broadcasting system as an integral addition to the nation's classroom facilities, as a way to make education exciting. He foresaw no reason why its advantages could not become a valuable American export—to all the classrooms of the world, so that no one need be out of touch with a potentially good learning device. Every child could be exposed to the great teachers of the world, as well as fine music, meaningful plays and literature, and "the whole fascinating range of human activity." But, he warned, while the Corporation for Public Broadcasting would receive part of its income from the federal government, it must be "carefully guarded from Government or from party control. It will be free, and it will be independent—and it will belong to all the people." What he envisioned then was a bank of knowledge, "Eventually . . . as valuable as the Federal Reserve Bank . . . . A wild and visionary idea? Not at all. Yesterday's strangest dreams are today's headlines." In the six years since, the nation's interest in the programs televised by the new facility has grown consistently. Particularly the public has followed the education network when it has shown, as Johnson promised, "public affairs [taking] place in view of all the citizens."

Ninetieth Congress of the United States of America

AT THE FIRST SESSION

*Begun and held at the City of Washington on Tuesday, the tenth day of January,
one thousand nine hundred and sixty-seven*

An Act

To amend the Communications Act of 1934 by extending and improving the
provisions thereof relating to grants for construction of educational television broadcasting facilities, by authorizing assistance in the construction
of noncommercial educational radio broadcasting facilities, by establishing
a nonprofit corporation to assist in establishing innovative educational
programs, to facilitate educational program availability, and to aid the
operation of educational broadcasting facilities; and to authorize a com-
prehensive study of instructional television and radio; and for other
purposes.

*Be it enacted by the Senate and House of Representatives of the
United States of America in Congress assembled,* That this Act may
be cited as the "Public Broadcasting Act of 1967".

TITLE I—CONSTRUCTION OF FACILITIES

EXTENSION OF DURATION OF CONSTRUCTION GRANTS FOR EDUCATIONAL BROADCASTING

SEC. 101. (a) Section 391 of the Communications Act of 1934 (47
U.S.C. 391) is amended by inserting after the first sentence the following new sentence: "There are also authorized to be appropriated for
carrying out the purposes of such section, $10,500,000 for the fiscal
year ending June 30, 1968, $12,500,000 for the fiscal year ending
June 30, 1969, and $15,000,000 for the fiscal year ending June 30, 1970."
(b) The last sentence of such section is amended by striking out
"July 1, 1968" and inserting in lieu thereof "July 1, 1971".

MAXIMUM ON GRANTS IN ANY STATE

SEC. 102. Effective with respect to grants made from appropriations for any fiscal year beginning after June 30, 1967, subsection (b)
of section 392 of the Communications Act of 1934 (47 U.S.C. 392(b))
is amended to read as follows:
"(b) The total of the grants made under this part from the appropriation for any fiscal year for the construction of noncommercial
educational television broadcasting facilities and noncommercial educational radio broadcasting facilities in any State may not exceed
8½ per centum of such appropriation."

NONCOMMERCIAL EDUCATIONAL RADIO BROADCASTING FACILITIES

SEC. 103. (a) Section 390 of the Communications Act of 1934 (47
U.S.C. 390) is amended by inserting "noncommercial" before "educational" and by inserting "or radio" after "television".
(b) Subsection (a) of section 392 of the Communications Act of
1934 (47 U.S.C. 392(a)) is amended by—
(1) inserting "noncommercial" before "educational" and by
inserting "or radio" after "television" in so much thereof as pre-
cedes paragraph (1);
(2) striking out clause (B) of such paragraph and inserting
in lieu thereof "(B) in the case of a project for television facilities,
the State noncommercial educational television agency or, in the
case of a project for radio facilities, the State educational radio
agency,";
(3) inserting "(i) in the case of a project for television facilities," and "noncommercial" before "educational"

THE 38TH YEAR – 1968

Traditionally the last year of a President's term is marked by a diminishing pace. Mostly the outgoing administration finishes wrapping its packages, making sure that everything is tidy. New starts, except for emergencies, are hardly considered. But Lyndon B. Johnson was no traditionalist. Nothing wound down; everyone and everything continued at breakneck speed almost till noon on Richard Nixon's Inauguration Day. The new legislation ran the gamut from an Indian Bill of Rights to a provision for school breakfasts, from Truth-in-Lending to Aircraft Noise Abatement, from a tax surcharge to the San Rafael and San Gabriel wildernesses and a Flaming Gorge recreational area, from guaranteed student loans to heart, cancer, and stroke programs, from Safe Streets to such trackless areas as North Cascades and Redwoods national parks, plus Scenic Rivers and Scenic Trails acts, and from the internationalism of Food for Peace to an act on Dangerous Drugs Control. It was a year in which Martin Luther King and Bobby Kennedy were murdered while the President pushed a recalcitrant Congress for gun controls. And a year in which Washington, D.C., rioted and burned in view of the White House while its prime resident refused to permit punitive arrests. Fifty-six landmark laws were enacted in a year in which a President could surprise and shock his citizens with the announcement that "With America's sons in the fields far away, with America's future under challenge right here at home, with our hopes and the world's hopes for peace in the balance every day, I do not believe that I should devote an hour or a day of my time to any personal partisan causes or to any duties other than the awesome duties of this office—the Presidency of your country.

"Accordingly, I shall not seek, and I will not accept, the nomination of my party for another term as your President."

Appropriately that last year saw the passage of the final act of the great civil rights trilogy designed by Johnson — the Fair Housing Act for which he had worked for three years. In January he had asked Congress to move a step closer to a true American goal: "the development of a national society in which the color of a man's skin is as irrelevant as the color of his eyes." He continued: "Racism—under whatever guise and whatever sponsorship—cannot be reconciled with the American faith." And when he signed the open housing bill the following mid-April, he observed, "I do not exaggerate when I say that the proudest moments of my Presidency have been times such as this when I have signed into law the promises of a century." As he would later say again and again, the Emancipation Proclamation of 1863 had been just that—a proclamation. The Civil Rights Acts of 1964, 1965, and 1968 were facts, foundation stones paving the way toward the eventual end of discrimination in human rights.

Ninetieth Congress of the United States of America

AT THE SECOND SESSION

Begun and held at the City of Washington on Monday, the fifteenth day of January, one thousand nine hundred and sixty-eight

An Act

To prescribe penalties for certain acts of violence or intimidation, and for other purposes.

Be it enacted by the Senate and House of Representatives of the United States of America in Congress assembled,

TITLE I—INTERFERENCE WITH FEDERALLY PROTECTED ACTIVITIES

SEC. 101. (a) That chapter 13, civil rights, title 18, United States Code, is amended by inserting immediately at the end thereof the following new section, to read as follows:

"§ 245. Federally protected activities

"(a)(1) Nothing in this section shall be construed as indicating an intent on the part of Congress to prevent any State, any possession or Commonwealth of the United States, or the District of Columbia, from exercising jurisdiction over any offense over which it would have jurisdiction in the absence of this section, nor shall anything in this section be construed as depriving State and local law enforcement authorities of responsibility for prosecuting acts that may be violations of this section and that are violations of State and local law. No prosecution of any offense described in this section shall be undertaken by the United States except upon the certification in writing of the Attorney General or the Deputy Attorney General that in his judgment a prosecution by the United States is in the public interest and necessary to secure substantial justice, which function of certification may not be delegated.

"(2) Nothing in this subsection shall be construed to limit the authority of Federal officers, or a Federal grand jury, to investigate possible violations of this section.

"(b) Whoever, whether or not acting under color of law, by force or threat of force willfully injures, intimidates or interferes with, or attempts to injure, intimidate or interfere with—

"(1) any person because he is or has been, or in order to intimidate such person or any other person or any class of persons from—

"(A) voting or qualifying to vote, qualifying or campaigning as a candidate for elective office, or qualifying or acting as a poll watcher, or any legally authorized election official, in any primary, special, or general election;

"(B) participating in or enjoying any benefit, service, privilege, program, facility, or activity provided or administered by the United States;

"(C) applying for or enjoying employment, or any perquisite thereof, by any agency of the United States;

"(D) serving, or attending upon any court in connection with possible service, as a grand or petit juror in any court of the United States;

"(E) participating in or enjoying the benefits of any program or activity receiving Federal financial assistance; or

"(2) any person because of his race, color, religion or national origin and because he is or has been—

"(A) enrolling in or attending any public school or public colleg_

THE 39TH YEAR – 1969

On the night of January 14, beginning shortly after 9 o'clock, Lyndon B. Johnson paid his official farewell to Washington in the same chamber where he had been introduced to Congress as a doorkeeper 38 years before. It was a sentimental evening, with grizzled legislators, cynical newsmen, and disciplined, beribboned generals crying openly. Never had Johnson been more eloquent, more deliberate. "Every President lives," he confided, "not only with what is, but with what has been and what could be." He spoke of the turbulence of the past five years, but he also reminded his auditors of the assets of the United States:

"—our economy,

"—the democratic system,

"—our sense of exploration . . .

"—the good commonsense and sound judgment of the American people, and

"—their essential love of justice."

In terms redolent of his Hill Country background he suggested that his administration represented a watershed "when there is—if not really a break with the past—at least the fulfillment of many of its oldest hopes, and a stepping forth into a new environment, to seek new goals . . . .

"We have finished a major part of the old agenda.

"Some of the laws that we wrote have already, in front of our eyes, taken on the flesh of achievement."

He went on to list those programs which had now become a part of American life—medicare, voting booths and housing open to all Americans, federal assistance to assure better schools, preschool education—Head Start, job training for the hard core unemployed, nearly full employment of the American working force, the setting aside of more millions of acres for the benefit of the American public. He spoke of what remained, especially the needs of the cities and the mitigation of life in the ghettos, protection against catastrophic illness for young and old, and the eventual elimination of "the paradox of poverty in the midst of plenty in this nation." Finally he concluded, somberly and soberly, emphasizing and savoring each phrase, with the words shown here:

"Now, it is time to leave. I hope it may be said, a hundred years from now, that by working together we helped to make our country more just, more just for all its people, as well as to insure and guarantee the blessings of liberty for all of our posterity.

"That is what I hope. But I believe that at least it will be said that we tried."

No one—*no one*—ever tried harder. The evidence was all in. The jury of future generations will deliver the ultimate judgment.

Now for 5 most demanding years in the White House, I have been strengthened by the counsel and the cooperation of two great former Presidents, Harry S. Truman and Dwight David Eisenhower. I have been guided by the memory of my pleasant and close association with the beloved John F. Kennedy, and with our greatest modern legislator, Speaker Sam Rayburn.

I have been assisted by my friend every step of the way, Vice President Hubert Humphrey. I am so grateful that I have been supported daily by the loyalty of Speaker McCormack and Majority Leader Albert.

I have benefited from the wisdom of Senator Mike Mansfield, and I am sure that I have avoided many dangerous pitfalls by the good commonsense counsel of the President Pro Tem of the Senate, Senator Richard Brevard Russell.

I have received the most generous cooperation from the leaders of the Republican Party in the Congress of the United States, Senator Dirksen and Congressman Gerald Ford, the Minority Leader.

No President should ask for more, although I did upon occasions. But few Presidents have ever been blessed with so much.

President-elect Nixon, in the days ahead, is going to need your understanding, just as I did. And he is entitled to have it. I hope every Member will remember that the burdens he will bear as our President, will be borne for all of us. Each of us should try not to increase these burdens for the sake of narrow personal or partisan advantage.

Now, it is time to leave. I hope it may be said, a hundred years from now, that by working together we helped to make our country more just, more just for all of its people, as well as to insure and guarantee the blessings of liberty for all of our posterity.

That is what I hope. But I believe that at least it will be said that we tried.

THE 40TH YEAR – 1970

Although Lyndon B. Johnson left Washington with its inter-mixture of triumphs and frustrations, he hardly retired. He advised fledging politicians, he turned football enthusiast, he worked his ranch, he wrote on his book, and he advised on the building of the library which was to house the papers of his times. Although he studiously avoided second-guessing his successor in the White House, he remained interested in the problems of the day and where possible acted as impartial teacher and preceptor in grappling with ideas and challenges. Thus he put together the seminar noted here, a combination of students and business leaders "rapping" under congenial circumstances. And with present and future students in mind he advised The University of Texas on the establishment of the Lyndon B. Johnson School of Public Affairs as a place where career government servants could be trained. Every student in the School, naturally enough, has been assigned a community service problem, from the sinking water table in the Texas Panhandle to the upgrading of teacher training in Central America. The students being trained might be bearded or mini-skirted, and definitely anti-establishment, but they had picked up the spoor pursued for decades by Lyndon Johnson.

Johnson Aides Criticize Nixon Policies

By MARTIN WALDRON

Special to The New York Times

STONEWALL, Tex., Aug. 28 —Two top economic advisers of the Johnson Administration aimed a low-key attack tonight at the economic policies of President Nixon.

Former President Lyndon B. Johnson made no direct criticism of President Nixon's Administration.

But Dr. Walter W. Heller, who was chairman of Mr. Johnson's Council of Economic Advisers, said that it was time for the current Administration "to stop riding the brake and start using the accelerator."

And Henry H. Fowler, the New York stockbroker who was Mr. Johnson's Secretary of the Treasury, said that a "massive budgetary deficit" as forecast by Mr. Nixon could seriously disrupt the stock market.

In introducing Mr. Fowler and Dr. Heller, who lectured at a seminar for about 200 Texas businessmen, bankers and students, Mr. Johnson said that the discussion was being held to try to gain some understanding of what lay ahead on the economic front.

"I hope we will temporarily suspend pointing the finger of blame," the former President said. "We only have one President and one economy, and we are all in this boat together."

Mr. Johnson posed a series of questions as a prelude to the lectures by his former advisers.

Several Questions Posed

"What can we do about our housing shortages?" he asked.

"I read somewhere the other day that a person who buys a $20,000 house today will pay $35,000 in interest over a 30-year period.

"Will interest rates go up or down? Will unemployment continue to rise? Will the rate of inflation decline?"

The two-hour seminar, held on a warm summer evening in the new Lyndon B. Johnson State Park across the Pedernales River from his LBJ Ranch home, was by invitation only.

Newsmen were barred, but the proceedings inside a new stone building in the park were piped outside through loudspeakers, and employes of the former President served beer and soft drinks to the newsmen.

Mr. Johnson, appearing to be 25 to 30 pounds heavier than when he was President, said that he planned several seminars at his ranch on "such subjects as environment, population control, food, health, beautification, arms limitation, education and foreign affairs."

The most vigorous comments on the economic policies of Mr. Nixon's Administration came from Dr. Heller, who said that he preferred to believe that President Nixon spoke in an "unguarded moment" when he recently said that prospects were that there would be full employment in this country by the end of next year.

Both he and Mr. Fowler said while it appeared that both interest rates and inflation had "peaked," unemployment would continue at this level or more in the next few years.

"The jobless rate bids fair to go up," said Dr. Heller, who is chairman of the department of economics at the University of Minnesota.

He gave two reasons: The failure of the economy's growth to keep pace with the increased number of workers from normal population increases, and the need for jobs for returning veterans from the Vietnam war.

The economist said that it would take a "miracle" to gain full employment in this country in the next 18 months, requiring a growth rate of more than 9 per cent a year.

But there is every indication, he said, that the nation "has turned the corner" on high interest rates, and that inflation could be slowed down to 3 per cent a year with the proper controls in Washington.

Both he and Mr. Fowler recommended that labor and management try to instill a sense of restraint in workers.

Mr. Fowler said that the projected deficit in next year's Federal budget must be held to a "modest" level to keep the money market strong.

"Any development that would make the Treasury a claimant for increasing amounts of borrowed money would preempt funds otherwise available for private investment or restoring corporate liquidity," Mr. Fowler said.

"This could also lead to a reversal in the recent encouraging decline in interest rates at least for the prime credit and the current stabilization of stock values at levels well above their May lows."

THE 41ST YEAR – 1971

The scriptural legacy of Lyndon B. Johnson lies in the Presidential Library that houses his papers. Thirty-plus million papers that tell the story of a sometimes frenetic, forever kinetic lifetime of public service. The cascade of activity increasingly affected the lives of every person in the United States, and whistled like the wind up the defiles and through the passes of even the remotest valleys and mountains of the world. Escape was as impossible as it would have been for a lone rider on the Staked Plains of Texas in the middle of a sleeting norther. But behind, for a more contemplative and digestive day, he left the papers—for generations of scholars who will examine and analyze, praise and criticize, and revise and re-revise for as long as men are interested in the gropings of the United States toward a more perfect union and in a never-ending pursuit of an indefinable happiness. In the library one can indeed find history "with the bark off."

The Library records reflect the Nation for 40 years -- from the
'30s through the '60s. They picture a sweep of history beginning with the
depression and ending with the most prosperous era we have ever known. They
record a drive for change and social reform unparalleled in its energy and
scope -- and a World War unmatched in its destruction. They chronicle the
end of colonialism -- and the beginning of the Cold War and the Atomic Age
which still threaten mankind. They cover the time when liberty was challenged in
Europe and Latin America and Asia -- and record America's response to
those challenges.

It is all here: the story of our time -- with the bark off.

A President sees things from a unique perspective. No one can share
his responsibility. No one can share the scope of his duties or the
burden of his decisions.

In my book, to be published this fall, I explain: "I have not written
these chapters to say, 'This is how it was,' but to say, 'This is how I
saw it from my vantage point.'"

This Library does not say, "This is how I saw it," but, "This
is how the documents show it was."

There is no record of a mistake, nothing critical, ugly, or unpleasant
that is not included in the files here. We have papers from my 40 years
of public service in one place, for friend and foe to judge, to approve or
to disapprove.

I donot know how this period will be regarded in years to come. But that
is not the point. This Library will show the facts...not just the joy and
triumphs, but the sorrow and failures, too.

THE 42ND YEAR – 1972

As the education and civil rights papers were opened at the Lyndon Baines Johnson Presidential Library, the tributes poured in. The former President, his physical pace slowed by pain while his spiritual and mental pace plunged on unabated, superintended the two-day ceremonies at each opening, and heard himself acclaimed by men he knew as the Education President and the Civil Rights President. Between times he prepared to depart his world, and with typical Johnson determination he delayed his exit till his preparations were complete. Almost his last accomplishment was to put the final touches on an act that had begun back in 1969, when his birthplace and boyhood home had been deeded to the National Park Service. Later the two Johnson homes had been dedicated to public enjoyment, as told on the adjoining page, and now in the last six weeks of his life he was turning over his rambling house and the heart of his beloved ranch to complete a unique National Historic Site. The Site is a jewel, for nowhere else in the United States is there such a complete portrait of a President's life—his birthplace, his romping area as a boy, his first country classroom, his high school, the postoffice where he mailed his first letter, the spot where he kissed his first girl, the store where he played dominoes, the ranch to which he brought the leaders of the world and to which he came home, the burial ground with its hovering oaks where he rests with his ancestors—all those and others within a dozen miles of one another. It was his last public service to his nation.

Two Johnson Homes Dedicated as Historic Sites

By MARTIN WALDRON
Special to The New York Times

JOHNSON CITY, Tex., June 13 —Secretary of the Interior Walter J. Hickel accepted for the nation this afternoon the titles to former President Lyndon B. Johnson's restored birthplace and to his boyhood home.

In ceremonies in 100 - degree heat under a sun that the former President said was "good for drying my hay," a crowd of 2,500 persons watched while Mr. Johnson and Gov. Preston Smith of Texas presented title to two acres of land and a small white frame house built to represent the farm home in which Mr. Johnson was born in 1908 and to the other house in town.

The National Park Service began maintaining the birthplace and the boyhood home here in January after Congress voted to designate both as historic sites. Formal dedication was postponed until today after the former President was hospitalized with symptoms of a heart attack.

The former President appeared to be in good health, although he did sound hoarse and a bit short of breath. He drove to the site of the cere-mony two miles from his ranch house in a restored 1910 Model T Ford, which was presented to him as a gift last year.

Mrs .Johnson, who was wearing a red and white print cotton dress, sat beside the former President holding their first grandchild, Patrick Lyndon Nugent. Mr. Johnson wore a navy blue wool suit and a red striped regimental tie.

An Air Force band flown yesterday from Langley, Va., played martial music before and during the ceremony.

Along the Pedernales

In accepting the two houses as historic sites, Mr. Hickel said that he was acting for President Nixon. Mr. Nixon sent a letter in which he praised Mr. Johnson as a man whose love for the southwest was "exceeded only by his love for his country."

The birthplace alongside the Pedernales River is surrounded at this time of the year by a host of Texas wildflowers, including three-foot tall yucca with its cream-colored blossoms and black-eyed susans.

Irrigation water pumped from the river keeps the lawns and pastures lush and green even though the site is the Texas hill country that has a limited amount of rain.

A small family cemetery surrounded by a red stone wall and shaded by large five oaks lies between the birthplace and the ranch house. Mr. Johnson's mother and father are buried there, and the former President has often said he wants to be buried in the family cemetery.

The birthplace was restored in 1966 by the Johnson City Foundation, formed by Mr. Johnson when he was still in the Senate. Roy White, an Austin architect, using photographs and suggestions from Mr. Johnson, designed a reproduction of the four-room farmhouse where the former President was born in 1908.

The birthplace is furnished in the fashion of the times. The kitchen contains a wood-burning stove and old fashioned food safe, a small table and several chairs. The bedroom contains some furniture that belonged to Mr. Johnson's mother and other pieces donated by friends of the family.

The boyhood home, about 15 miles from the birthplace, is similarly furnished. Built in 1886, it is a semi-Victorian frame structure that was also reconstucted to some degree after Mr. Johnson became President.

Mr. Johnson's father moved his family into Johnson City during World War I and in 1922 sold his share of the family ranch, which had been bought in 1882 by Mr. Johnson's grandmother. She had sold a silver-mounted carriage and a matched span of horses, which had been a present from her brother, to get a down payment. She taught school to make the monthly payments on the 950 acres.

In 1951, when he was in the Senate, Mr. Johnson began buying back the family homestead, including the ranch house, which he enlarged to include nine bathrooms.

Mr. Johnson bought much of the land from his aunt, Mrs. Clarence Martin.

The birthplace is the first piece of Mr. Johnson's LBJ Ranch to become public property. Many of the former President's friends have said that it is Mr. Johnson's intention to will the entire ranch to the Federal Government.

THE 43RD YEAR – 1973

When Lyndon B. Johnson died, just as his successor began his second term and uncertain peace came to Vietnam, the world paid tribute. In all the outpouring of praise or critical evaluation, none caught the spirit of Johnson so well as a former assistant, Horace Busby, who had worked for and with Johnson intermittently from the middle 1940's to the day of his death, and, like so many of Johnson's associates, remained always on call.

LBJ Toward the End: Getting Things in Order

Horace Busby, a native of Fort Worth, was associated with Lyndon B. Johnson at intervals from the time Johnson entered the Senate until shortly before his death. He was press secretary and general handyman for LBJ during the Senate days, was secretary to the cabinet and special assistant in the White House during part of the LBJ presidency.

BY HORACE BUSBY

©1973, Los Angeles Times-
Washington Post News Service

On Sunday, Dec. 31, 1972, at my home in the Washington suburbs, I was awakened early in the morning by the telephone. When I answered, a Secret Service agent at the ranch in Texas announced: "President Johnson is calling."

Over 25 years, countless days had begun in much the same way, for me and for all other former assistants from the early years whom Lyndon Johnson liked to call "my boys."

Whatever his office — congressman, senator, vice-president or president — he was awake at dawn, thinking out his strategies to surmount what others deemed insurmountable. Once his plans were set, he reached for the telephone and, oblivious to the hour, began launching his characteristic counterattack on the approaching day. The pattern lingered on in retirement.

If the call were typical, his manner on this morning was not. He did not banter casually. Speaking crisply and, it seemed, rather hurriedly, he went directly to his point.

"I've called," he said, "about two things."

Out of old habit, I picked up a pencil and prepared to take notes. He did not continue. I heard him lay down the telephone — and there were sounds of glasses clinking and water being poured. A minute or more passed before he spoke again.

"I'm swallowing these nitro-glycerin pills," he said matter-of-factly, "like a goldfish gulping crackers."

While he did not always take kindly to inquiries about his health, I ventured a question anyway, asking how he had been feeling.

"Just fair," he replied. "I'm trying to get in better shape so the doctors will let me go to Mexico next month and rest up in the Sun. But it's not good."

The answer was unexpected. Only the previous day, news accounts reported President and Mrs. Johnson's attendance at memorial services in Austin for 16 teen-agers who died in a holiday traffic tragedy. I had assumed his presence at those services meant his health must be improved.

When I began mentioning the news reports, however, he immediately bridled. He apparently suspected that I meant to reproach him—as others around him had been doing in recent weeks—for attending too many funerals, each of which seemed to take a deep emotional toll. He cut my comment short.

"Now, Buzz," he said firmly, "you've got to understand those families all live in South Austin."

In the context of his career, that was explanation enough. Since 1937, when he first ran for Congress, Lyndon Johnson had never fully come to terms with Austin's proud old family elite—"the better people," as they were known in the class-conscious New Deal era—who lived in the palatial early century homes of North Austin.

They resented him politically and were contemptuous of him socially: He was born wrong, schooled wrong, had wrong friends, wrong interests and wrong style. But across the river, in the modest homes of South Austin where the "little people" lived, he always had the votes.

That schism marked the man from the beginning to the end of his public life. While the fires within him had long been banked, now an ember began to glow hot inside.

"Those people," he said with sudden intensity, "are my people. When nobody else was with me, they stood by me. When they hurt, I hurt. Nothing"—he repeated the word twice more—"is ever going to keep me away from them in times like they're going through."

I said no more about funerals.

To Cease-Fire

After a moment, he turned the conversation, raising the subject of the Vietnam cease-fire negotiations.

"I think they've about got it," he said, "or they will have it soon. I just pray to God they can make it stick."

He continued on, repeating concerns he frequently expressed for what might happen next in other Asian lands. Although his comments were not optimistic, he was talking now about national concerns and his mood brightened noticeably and the horizons of the conversation expanded to Congress, the new cabinet appointments, economic policy.

"Be sure," he told me, "to meet Barbara Jordan." The newly elected black congresswoman from Texas greatly impressed him. "She's one of the best," he said, "to go up the pike from down here in a long time."

Other such directions came tumbling out as he went along. There were two editorial page articles in recent issues of the Washington Post which he wanted me to read, "think about," and send him a memorandum of comment. He would like to have any statistics I could find about black voting in the 1972 national elections. The indicated low turnout of both blacks and 18-year-olds was, he thought, "a damn disgrace." When he returned from Mexico in March, he added, "we've got to get some smart people together and try to figure out something to change that before the next election."

For Lectures

In this mood, he skipped to another pet project. He was trying, he reported, to raise $1 million to fund a guest lectureship program at the library in Austin. But he was dissatisfied with the current "crop" of lecturers touring the campus circuit.

"Some of those faces," he said, "are getting pretty old and tiresome. Their needles have been stuck for 10 years. Aren't there any new and exciting thinkers!"

I began suggesting some Washington figures, but he interrupted. "Hell," he said, "nobody there has enough charisma to fill a small phone booth, except Kissinger, and he's always someplace else."

I laughed, of course, at this flash of his typical humor, and he ran through a list of other names offering similar succinct comments on each. Then, serious again, he added another assignment.

"While I'm gone," he said, "talk to some good people up there and get some names of lecturers who can really shake up things. These kids on campus aren't fired up like they ought to be."

This talk reminded him of another campus matter. He had been invited, he reported, to deliver the commencement address at the University of Virginia when his son-in-law, Charles Robb, received his law degree this spring.

Less Typical

"That's an old school, a fine school," he commented, "and I want to make the best speech of my life. Remember," he went on, "when Thomas Jefferson wrote his own epitaph, he asked that his tombstone say he was a founder of the University of Virginia."

The mood was upbeat, even soaring. This had become a typical early morning Lyndon Johnson conversation. Abruptly, though, he left the telephone once again as he had done at the beginning of the call. When he resumed, nothing was said to explain the interruption, but he returned to his opening remark.

"One of the things I wanted to say," he began, "is that I am very pleased with what we've been able to accomplish

"SEPTEMBER SONG"

[On September 16, 1972, four months before his death, Lyndon B. Johnson spoke at the 75th anniversary of a Temple, Texas, hospital, the Scott and White Clinic. He was walking slowly now, and the nitroglycerin pill was ever handy. The speech he made that evening was philosophical, but as sometimes happens, its application became immediate. In the months since Johnson's death the travails of the nation have deepened the September mood of which he spoke, so that the battle between the winter of discontent now upon the land and the spring of optimism for what may yet emerge seems even more crucial than when Johnson made these comments.]

With the coming of September each year, we are reminded, as the song says, that the days are dwindling down to a precious few. By the calendar, we know that soon the green leaves of summer will begin to brown; the chill winds of winter will begin to blow; and—before we are ready for the end to come—the year will be gone.

If we permit our thoughts to dwell upon this perspective, these days can become a melancholy season.

As it is with the calendar, so it sometimes seems to be with our country and our system. For there are those among us who would have us believe that America has come to its own September. That our days are dwindling down to a precious few. That the green leaves of our best season are turning brown and soon will be falling to the ground. That before long we will feel the first chill winds of a long American winter—and that our nation's span as mankind's "last best hope" will be done.

For those who preach this prophecy—and for those who believe it—this period of our affairs can only be a melancholy season. But it is to that mood—and to the perceptions which foster it—that I want to address my remarks today.

Over the course of a long, full and gratifying life, I have seen many Septembers and known many autumns. In public service—and in private life—I have experienced a full measure of unwelcome winters. Yet melancholy is not a mood which I have ever allowed to weigh for long upon my spirits.

I live—as I have always worked—by the faith that with each passing day, we are always approaching nearer to the beginning of a new springtime.

It is by that perspective I see our country now.

If I believe anything of this land—if I know anything of its people and their character—I believe and I know that we have not come to and are not approaching America's September.

On the contrary, it is my conviction—a conviction which deepens every day—that this land and its people are quickening with the new life and new potential of what will become the springtime of a new America.

I do not say this merely to offer reassurance in anxious times. Far from it, I intend what I say to be taken as a challenge—a challenge to every citizen of every age.

No nation can be more than the visions of its people. America cannot be more than we believe ourselves capable of becoming. Thus we are directly challenged to choose between two very different perceptions of what we are and what we can make of America itself.

On the one hand, we can choose to guide our course by the light of the bright perceptions—of America the beautiful, America the just, America the land of the free and the home of the brave.

Or, on the other hand, we can choose to move toward the shadows of what some have called "the dark perception"—of America the unclean, America the unjust, America the unworthy.

For myself—as, I am sure, for many of you—there is no real choice. I want to open the soul of America to the warm sunlight of faith in itself, faith in the principles and precepts of its birth, faith in the promise and potential of its resources and skills and people. Yet I know that, in these times, this is not easy.

For too long, we have permitted the dark perception to pervade our midst. Day after day, month after month, the portrayal of America as unclean, unjust and unworthy has been ground into the consciousness of our people.

We no longer see the blooming flowers for we are searching for the litter. We no longer celebrate the many fresh triumphs of justice for we are lingering over the residue of yesterday's shortcomings. We no longer measure the miles we have come toward a more humane, civil and peaceful world for we are too busy calibrating the remaining inches of times we are trying to escape and leave behind.

This is our clear and present challenge.

When we permit these dark perceptions to dominate us, we are allowing our future to be shaped by visions that are small and mean and diminishing to our potential. We are, in simple terms, dooming those who come after us to know what could only be a second-rate America.

This is a future which I am unwilling to accept.

I have devoted my time on this earth to working toward the day when there would be no second-class citizenship in America, no second-quality opportunity, no second-hand justice at home, no second-place status in the world for our ideals and beliefs.

I do not intend now that second-rate visions shall set our course toward settling for a second-rate America.

That is why I speak as I do now.

All through the pages of history—and nowhere more than in the history of medicine—we read the heart-rending stories of those who set out in quest of great goals and discoveries, yet when they were almost to the edge of success, they hesitated—not knowing or understanding how near they were to their aims. Out of that moment of hesitation, all too often they lost forever their opportunity to succeed.

In many respects, that seems to me to be a pattern we ourselves are in danger of repeating.

Over all the years of our nation's existence, we have been setting goals for ourselves and striving tirelessly to reach them. Those goals have been both the slogans and the substance of national affairs for generation after generation.

Full employment. Decent wages. Adequate housing.

Education for everyone. Opportunity for all.

Good health, good medical care, good hospitals for even the least among us.

Above all, equal justice under the law for all our fellow men.

America's goals have been simple and basic.

They have permeated and motivated all our institutions—churches and schools and professions and labor unions and corporations and foundations—as well as our governments at every level.

All our American resources and strengths—private and public—have been committed to the effort and we have come very close to success.

Nowhere—over all the globe—have any people, under

any other system, come nearer to fulfillment of such aspirations than have we under our system.

Yet, at the very moment we were near to realization, we have allowed our effort to go slack, our momentum to slow and we have entered a season of hesitation.

Why?

Basically, I believe, it is because we have not understood—and still do not fully comprehend—where we are or what we are about.

Let me illustrate with one example.

Since the early Presidency of Thomas Jefferson, this nation has been committed—as no other nation on earth—to education of all our children. We have valued the minds of our young as America's richest resource and we have honored that value by dedicating much of our wealth to development of those minds. Our purpose has been not to provide education for education's sake, but to equip our young people to be agents of change—questioning the past, challenging the status quo, changing the prospects of the human condition.

In our own very recent times, this long sustained national effort has come to fruition. Never before in any society have there been so many educated men and women—or so many young people enrolled in pursuit of education. Yet when we came face to face with young people who were questioning the past, who were challenging the status quo, who were working to change the prospects of the human condition—we have hesitated in doubt and sometimes in fear of the educated young.

Across the full breadth of our national efforts, I could repeat countless other parallels. Out of the very success of our system have come the qualms and doubts that contribute to the melancholy of this season.

Whatever may be your own perception of where we are and where we may be tending, let me say for myself that I see little today suggesting that our system is failing—but I see all too much which convincingly argues that by our doubts and hesitation we may be failing the promise and potential of our system.

Our forefathers—all those before us—set in motion a system which would achieve change. The fruits of their efforts—and of their visions—have ripened in our times. Old values, old standards and old meanings have yielded to change. So have the old arrangements and old relationships by which others lived. We have perceived all this as signals and symptoms of a world in collapse. And with that perception, we have become susceptible to any and all who suggest that for our system, the days are dwindling down to a precious few.

But I argue that this is not reality.

We are not living in times of collapse. The old is not coming down. Rather, the troubling and torment of these days stems from the new trying to rise into place.

With our nation's past efforts, with our long and faithfully kept commitments, with our infinite successes in so many fields, we have brought into being the materials, as it were, with which to construct a new America.

We are not caretakers of the past. We are contractors charged with the construction of tomorrow.

Faced with a task of such great dimensions, we have no time for melancholy. We have no cause for moroseness. We have work to be done—the greatest work any generation of Americans has ever faced. Believing that, I say—let's be on with our labors.

The foundations are already in place, solid and secure.

We have beneath us the sturdy footing of the Bill of Rights—and it does not need us to be tinkering or tampering with it.

We have supporting us the strength and compassion of our great religious and ethical heritage—and that heritage does not need us to be denying it.

We have working for us the many decades of toil and labor invested in this system by earlier generations—and that investment does not need us to squander it by refusing or failing to invest our own toil and labor today.

The essentials of a new America—a better America—are all on hand and within our reach. It is our destiny—and, I believe, our duty—to take up our appointed positions and commence the labors that will change what needs change among us.

Our real challenge lies not in suppressing change but in utilizing it to vitalize and energize our society. Change is not our enemy. On the contrary, this society has no deadlier danger than refusal to change.

That is what I believe our young Americans are trying—and have been trying—to communicate to us. With their fine young minds, fresh new learning and clear new vision, they are seeing many segments of our society as it needs to be seen and understood.

They are telling us that government must change, business must change, medicine must change, labor must change, law must change—change not to depart from our system's principles but change to honor and keep those principles in new times.

A society engaged in the tasks of change will not long linger at the feet of those who preach that its days are dwindling down to only a precious few. A society caught up in the toil and sweat—in the thrill and excitement—of its own confident visions will not be drawn into the melancholy of dark perceptions.

At the risk of repetition—but in an effort to assure there is no misunderstanding of my purpose—let me summarize my message to you this way:

—This nation came into being because people wanted change.

—We went through some dangerous periods, but we have emerged with the best system that men have devised on earth.

—We need not, and we must not, chip away at the granite foundations on which our system is built . . . the freedoms guaranteed in our constitution and the new opportunities achieved in our own time.

—But this is not to deny that the system itself needs improvements, to meet the demands of a new day.

—Change and improvement can and will come. But it must not and cannot be change built on an effort to depict us falsely as a selfish, decadent and greedy land.

—The most frightening thing that could happen to us today would be for us to close our eyes to new ideas, and close our ears to those—particularly the young, in whom we have invested so much hope and effort through the years of our existence—who are trying to tell us how they would go about perfecting the visions of America the beautiful, America the just, America the land of the free and home of the brave. At the same time, we must help them restore the reality of America the busy, America the active, America the land of the confident and the home of the courageous.

It is just such spirit that we honor on this occasion. It is by restoring that spirit to our lives and our nation's life we can honor our own trust as Americans.

While President Johnson's body lay in state inside, huge lines snaked outside—beyond the LBJ Library, through the adjoining Sid Richardson Building, and into the vast parking lot beyond. One enterprising historian went among the people with a tape recorder, gathering people's thoughts as they waited on that cold January day and night. Among the varied answers was this one-sentence observation from an elderly man which pretty well sums up the attitude of Johnson watchers through the generations:

*"He stood high, he walked handsome, and he
was a one hundred per cent gentleman."*

"Okay, George Christian, wherever you are.

You were right. We miss him."